Disclaimer

The information included in this book is designed to provide helpful information on the subjects discussed. This book is not meant to be used to diagnose or treat any medical condition. For diagnosis or treatment of any medical problem, consult your own doctor. The author and publisher are not responsible for any specific health or allergy needs that may require medical supervision and are not liable for any damages or negative consequences from any application, action, treatment, or preparation, to anyone reading or following the information in this book. Links may change and any references included are provided for informational purposes only.

D0731409

Crafting

The Top 300 Best Crafts
Fun and Easy Crafting Ideas, Patterns, Hobbies, Jewelry and More For You, Family, Friends and Holidays

By Susan Hollister
Copyright © 2017

Table of Contents

Introduction   15

Chapter 1: Set Up Your Craft Area   17

Organization is Key...17

Workspace 18

Storage..18

Shelving...19

Tips...20

Finding Supplies 21

The Crafts...21

Chapter 2: Fabric Crafts   23

Drawstring Bag...23

Fabric Bookmark 24

Fabric-Covered Bins 25

Fabric-Covered Bulletin Board 27

Fabric-Covered Lampshade...27

Fabric-Covered Notebook 29

Fabric Headband 30

Fabric Heating Pad 31

Fabric Keychain 31

Fabric Scrunchie 32

Fabric-Covered Switch Plate 34

Felt Animals 35

Felt Coasters 36

Felt Heart Ornaments 37

Felt Play Mat 39

Framed Wall Hanging..40

Hot Pad 41

No-Sew Accent Pillow 42

No-Sew Blankets 44

Oven Mitts 45

Pillowcase 46

Tablecloth 47

Quilt Block Wall Hanging..48

Sleep Pillow 50

Sunglasses Case 51

Wall Hangings 52

Chapter 3: Scrapbooking — 54

Scrapbook Page Design 54

Theme-Based Scrapbooking....................................56

Art Scrapbook 57

Baby Scrapbook 58

Bucket List Scrapbook 58

Diary Scrapbook 58

Family Tree Scrapbook...59

Favorite Quote Scrapbook 60

Foodie Scrapbook 60

Gardening Scrapbook...60

Gift Scrapbook 61

Goals Scrapbook 61

Holiday Scrapbook 62

Love Letter Scrapbook 62

Medical Scrapbook...63

Nature Scrapbook 63

Party Scrapbook 64

Pet Scrapbook 65

Positive Affirmation Scrapbook................................66

Schooldays Scrapbook 66
Seashore Scrapbook.....................................68
Storytelling Scrapbooks...............................69
Thankfulness Scrapbook 69
To The Bride Scrapbook 70
Travel Scrapbook..71
Year-In-Review Scrapbook 72

Chapter 4: Painting Crafts 73

Tips For Painting...73
Canvas Wall Hangings 74
Dripped Canvas Wall Hanging 76
Painted Accent Pillow 77
Painted Apron 77
Painted Bird House 78
Painted Canvas Shoes 79
Painted Clay Flower Pots..............................81
Painted Glass Jars..82
Painted Glass Plates 83
Painted Pail/Watering Can 84
Painted Plastic Tub.......................................85
Painted Stair Risers 86
Painted Tote Bag..87
Painted Two-Liter Bottle Butterflies.............88
Painted Tin Cans..89
Painted Rocks...90
Pallet Sign Post..91
Pallet Wall Hanging 92
Repurposed, Painted Baby Wipes Containers 93
Small Pallet Wall Hanging 93

Spattered Stained Glass Vase.................................94

Spray-Painted Circle Art 95

Striped Painted Initials Letters 96

Swirled Stained Glass Vase...................................96

Watercolor Phrase Wall Hanging 97

Chapter 5: Fragrant Crafts   99

CANDLEMAKING 99

A Word About Wax 99

The Basics Of Molded Candles 100

Canning Jar Luminaries 101

Glass Jar Candles 102

Layered Glass Candle 103

Painted Pillars 104

Paper Napkin Candle...104

Paper Napkin Candle, Alternative Method 105

Pressed Flower And Herbs Glass Candle 106

Teacup Candle..106

SOAP 107

Herb Lemon Soap..107

Lavender Rosemary Bars......................................108

Lemon Soap 109

Oatmeal Soap...109

Pumpkin Pie Soap 110

SCRUBS 111

Coffee Scrub...111

Lavender Scrub 111

Lemon Scrub 112

Mint Sugar Scrub..112

Sugar Olive Oil Scrub..113

FRAGRANCES...113

Baking Soda Scent 113

Gel Diffuser 114

Rice Diffuser 115

Wood Block Diffuser 116

POTPOURRI..116

Crock-Pot Potpourri 116

Rose Spice Potpourri 118

Simmering Potpourri....................................118

Chapter 6: Wood Crafts   **120**

Balsa Book Cover...120

Balsa Wood Bookmark 121

Chalkboard Town 123

Craft Stick Jewelry Box 124

Craft Stick Potpourri Box 124

Crafting With Wooden Cutouts.......................125

Cutting Board 125

Decorated Wooden Letters............................127

Decorative Checkerboard 128

Front Door Welcome Hanger 129

Hexagonal Basket 130

Fairy Door 131

Jewelry Holder 132

Lost Sock Holder 133

Miniature Village..134

Pallet Headboard 135

Pallet Wall Hanging 136

Pallet Flag...136

Pine Coasters 137

Pine Hot Pads...138

Scrap Wood Wall Art...139

Storage Crates...140

Wall Coat Rack...141

Walking Stick...142

Wood Burned Coasters And Hot Pads..........................143

Wood Burned Picture Frame..144

Chapter 7: Sculpting and Modeling 145

Types Of Clay 145

Polymer clay...145

Air-dry clay...146

Natural earth clay 146

Salt clay..146

Paper mache clay 147

Baking soda clay..147

Clay Projects...148

Air-Drying Clay Tealight Holder 148

Architectural Designs 149

Baking Soda Clay Pressed-Flower Hangings 149

Clay-Covered Jars..151

Clay-Covered Thumbtacks...151

Colored And Waxed Salt Clay Hangers.........................152

Crochet Hook Covers 154

Colored Pencil Holder 155

Country Window Hanger 156

Decorative Mask 156

Paper Mache Clay Butterfly 157

Paper Mache Village 159

Polymer Clay Covered Cans...160

Polymer Clay Cupboard Knobs 160
Polymer Clay Coasters...161
Polymer Clay Garden Markers 162
Polymer Clay Pen Covers.......................................163
Polymer Clay Trinket Bowl 164
Salt Dough Doilies 165
Salt Clay Pet Print Memorials................................166
Salt Dough Picture Frame......................................167
Salt Dough Rainbow 169
Salt Clay Animals 170
Stamped Clay Wall Hangings.................................171

Chapter 8: Tape Crafting   173

Duct Tape Bookmark..174
Duct Tape Clutch...174
Duct Tape Drawer Organizer 176
Duct Tape Frame...176
Duct Tape Key Chain 177
Duct Tape Lanyard 177
Duct Tape Refrigerator Magnet 178
Duct Tape Rose Pens 179
Duct Tape Tablet Cover 180
Duct Tape Tote Bag...181
Duct Tape Wall Hangings 182
Duct Tape Wallet 183
Washi Tape Binder Clips...185
Washi Tape Coasters...185
Washi Tape Chopsticks 186
Washi Tape Flower Pot 186
Washi Tape Gift Tags...187

Washi Tape Monogram Wall Hanging 188

Washi Tape Notebook 189

Washi Tape Pens 189

Washi Tape Phone Cover 190

Washi Tape Photo Frames 190

Washi Tape Sunglasses 191

Washi Tape Switchplate 192

Washi Tape Vase 193

Chapter 9: Button Crafts   194

Button Greeting Cards 195

Autumn Tree Wall Hanging 196

Button Bookmark 196

Button Bowl 197

Button Bracelet 198

Button Calendar 199

Button Cars 200

Button Clock 201

Button-Encrusted Vase 202

Button Keychain 202

Button Lampshade 203

Button Magnet 204

Button Magnets With Clothespin Holders 204

Button Napkin Rings 205

Button Pencil Holders 205

Button Picture Frame 206

Button Pillows 207

Button Purse 208

Button-Rimmed Flowerpot 208

Button Thumbtacks 209

Button Welcome Wreath 209

Button Wreath On Canvas 210

Button Monogram 212

Cute-As-A-Button Hair Clip.......................................213

Embroidered Napkins With Buttons 213

Chapter 10: Making Jewelry   **214**

Adjustable Wire Charm Bangle Bracelet 215

Woven T-Shirt Bracelet 216

Ball Chain Ring 217

Button Pendant 218

Charm Ring...218

Crocheted Bracelet 219

Headpin Earring 220

Hoop Earring 221

Leather Bead Ring 223

Nail Polish Pendant 224

Paint Chip Earrings 224

Pearl Teardrop Earrings 226

Polymer Clay Swirl Pendant 227

Popsicle Stick Bracelet 228

Seashell Pendant..229

Soda Can Ribbon Bracelet 230

Tassel Earrings 232

Washer Necklace 233

Washi Tape Earrings...235

Washi Tape Popsicle Stick Bracelet 236

Washi Tape Washer Necklace 237

Wired Button Ring 238

Wire Shank Button Ring 239

Wire-wrapped Rings 241
Wire-Wrapped Stone Or Sea-Glass Pendant 242

Chapter 11: Yarn Crafts 243

Crochet-Covered Hanger..245
Crochet-Enhanced Flip-flops 246
Eye Of God 247
Pompom Bookmark 248
Spiral Yarn Wall Hanging 249
Woven Butterfly...250
Yarn Basket 251
Yarn Bowl 252
Yarn Dolls 253
Yarn Globes...254
Yarn Wall Hanging 256
Yarn Wall Hanging 2 257
Yarn-Wrapped Desk Accessories.............................257
Yarn-Wrapped Flowerpot 258

Chapter 12: Kid-Friendly Family Crafts 260

Button Tree Canvas For Kids 260
Clay Flowers..260
Coffee Filter Ornamental Bowls 261
Craft Stick Frame...262
Clothespin Clamps...263
Clothespin Car Air Fresheners 264
Felt Flower Bookmark 265
Foam Shape Wreath 265
Glove Monsters..266
Handprint Salt Clay Bird 267
Knot Ring..268

Magazine People...269

Magic Wands 270

Paper Bead Necklace...271

Pet Bugs 272

Picture Frame Sun-Catcher 273

Polymer Clay Key Chain......................................274

Polymer Clay Window Ornaments 274

Rainbow Suncatcher 275

Rainstick...276

Sun Catcher Lids...277

Tic Tac Tote 278

Tin Can Mobile..279

Twig Frame 280

Wooden Utensils, Decorated 281

Chapter 13: Holiday Crafts   283

Burlap Silverware Holders..................................283

Button Christmas Tree 284

Canning Ring Pumpkin 285

Clothespin Turkeys..286

Craft Stick Halloween Spider 287

Craft Stick Star Of David 288

Delicate Designs On Dyed Easter Eggs 289

Easter-inspired Jar...289

Easy Homemade Menorah With Glass Votive Candles
....290

Egg Carton Easter Containers..............................291

Felt And Button Feather Tree..............................292

Firecracker Favors 294

Ghost In A Jar 295

Holiday Accent Pillow Covers 297
Paint Chip Ornaments 298
Paper Heart Valentine's Day Wreath 299
Patriotic Circle Fans 301
Patriotic Jar Luminaries 302
Peppermint Bowls 303
Ribbon Christmas Tree Ornament 304
Salt Clay Snowman Keepsake Ornament 305
Paint Chip Easter Egg Garland 307
Unique Valentine In A Bottle 308
Wine Glass Snow Globe Candleholder 309

Conclusion 310

My Other Books 311

Introduction

Get prepared for hours of fun crafting adventures.

In this book of over 300 different crafts ideas, you will find clear steps and instructions for making all kinds of different beautiful crafts. You can sell them, give them to friends, or use them to decorate your home.

The crafts in this book are designed with enjoyment and beauty in mind. Each craft comes with a list of necessary items and detailed instructions to make the process as simple as possible. Learn how to make crafts with fabric – you won't even need to know how to sew! I'll show you how to put together a scrapbook, then you can fill it to the brim with memories. Learn how to paint on canvas or wood, creating colorful items that delight all who see them.

You'll also learn how you can make soap, candles, and other sources of pleasant fragrance. Learn to carve items from wood or soap and sculpt them with clay. Complete easy and fun crafts using washi tape and buttons. Have fun making amazing jewelry, designing it specifically for the person who will wear it. Discover many ways to use yarn, starting with crocheting and knitting. I've included plenty of fun crafts for kids of all ages and even decorations for different holidays.

It is a well-known truth that crafting can bring you peace of mind and can unleash your innate creativity. A creative mind is a happy mind, so crafting can contribute to your mental health. It will also exercise your brain, keeping it sharp and alert.

Crafting can relieve the stresses of life and help you relax. It can help you calm yourself and can ease anxiety. After all, there are no rules with crafting, so there's no pressure to perform. Many crafts can be completed in a short amount of time, so if you start to feel restless and bored, give yourself the pleasure of playing with a craft! It'll provide stress relief and a nice confidence boost when the project is done.

Crafting can set the stage for a satisfying life by stirring up your creativity. Teach your children to craft and you will build their self-confidence, while they develop fine motor skills and come up with new problem-solving strategies.

You can sell your crafts to make a little money, make them just for your own amusement, or give them away. Crafts make great gifts for the holidays. You can even make your own holiday décor. With over 300 crafts in the following these pages, you're sure to find something to suit your mood, anytime.

Chapter 1: Set Up Your Craft Area

Few people have the luxury of an entire room set aside for the storage and making of crafts. It's much more common to store your supplies in a closet, a basement, or a garage. More often than not, the dining room table becomes a crafter's workbench.

I grew up in a home where crafting was the norm. It was a rare occasion when my family actually ate at the dining room table. Most of the time, the table was covered with paint and canvas, little wooden objects, patterns for sweaters and hats, or jewelry findings. Everything was cleared off for holiday dinners or when guests came to call, but then you had to scramble to find what you had been working on.

While this works well for some people, it really helps to have a place to store craft supplies and – if you can swing it – a separate work space devoted to crafting. In this chapter, we will discuss several ways you can store your craft supplies without losing them when guests come over for dinner. We'll also talk about things every crafter should own and how to keep things organized, so you can find them when you need them.

Organization is Key

The two most important things a crafter needs are appropriately sized storage containers and a way to label them. If you participate in several forms of crafts, and many crafters do, you can assign each craft a different color of label, so you can easily access what you need for any given project. Whatever you do, don't procrastinate when it comes to organizing your crafts. If you organize as you go along, you'll be able to put your fingers on anything you need. If you overlook this critical task, you will swiftly become buried in random chaos and find yourself buying duplicate items unnecessarily.

Workspace

Generally speaking, the type of crafts you are involved in will determine the type of workspace you need. Crochet and needlework can usually be done on your lap; that's why so many people take them wherever they go. They're easy to pull out and work on in odd moments.

Other crafts will require a more elaborate setup. Quilting may require a large space in which to place the frame. Leather tooling and metalwork both call for a solid surface that can withstand hammering. Painting may require a table or an easel. Fine beadwork, on the other hand, may require little more than a storage chest to organize the beads and a relatively small flat surface on which to work.

If you're just starting out, you may not know what sort of workspace you will need for your craft. It's perfectly okay to learn as you go. Over time, you will develop your own workspace and you'll establish an organizational system that works best for you.

When you're working from a kit or an instruction booklet, these will usually list up front what equipment you will need before you can start a project. Each craft in this book will tell you at the outset which tools and what equipment you will need; this will give you an idea of how much space the craft will require.

You will also want to check the lighting where you plan to work. Will it be adequate, or do you need to add lamps to the area? In addition, some crafts can be quite messy; do you need a sink nearby for cleanup? If so, take this into account when deciding on your workspace.

Storage

One of the important steps in creating a craft area is deciding what kind of storage containers you want to use. Plastic tubs come in a variety of shapes and sizes. I recommend storing Christmas crafts in red and green-colored tubs and Halloween crafts in orange or black tubs. On the other hand, clear tubs make it easy to see what's inside. Nevertheless, you'll want to stay consistent with your labeling.

You can obviously use cardboard boxes for short-term storage. I emphasize short-term storage because these can easily wick moisture and odors into the inside, allowing mold and insects to grow. They do not provide the tighter seal offered by plastic totes. Stacking can also be a problem with cardboard, because excessive weight may cause them to collapse. Believe me, the last thing you want is a crafting avalanche!

Craft manufacturers have come up with ingenious ways to store craft items. Beads, jewelry findings, and other tiny supplies are easily stored in plastic boxes with dividers to keep each type of bead separated. They close tightly so that, even when dropped, the items in the little compartments will not mix. Rolling, stackable drawers are also available, allowing you to move your supplies to wherever you want to work. Photo storage boxes are inexpensive and work well to store many small items.

Shelving

Shelving might be just the thing you need for managing larger craft items. If you are using a bedroom as your craft room, check the closet. Do you need all that space to hang clothes? If not, add some shelving to hold bins and boxes. If you are storing items in a basement or a garage, stack your supplies up off the floor. Pallets are readily available – I have even included a section on how to use pallets for a variety of crafts. You can use the pallets for storage risers until you need to use them for your next craft project.

If this all sounds a little overwhelming and expensive, do not fret. You can make your own storage containers for a fraction of the cost of new ones. You can use clean tin cans for storage of colored pencils, paintbrushes, rulers and other drawing supplies. Empty baby food jars are great for storing little things like beads, buttons, knitting markers, clips, jewelry bead, and such. Plastic butter tubs can store a wealth of craft products from sewing bobbins and thread to embroidery thread, nails, and screws. If you have the space, attach a pegboard to a wall where you can hang tools within easy reach. An old filing cabinet can serve to store canvas, drawing paper, tissue paper or scrapbook papers. Just stash the paper in manila file folders so it doesn't get wrinkled.

Tips

These tips can help you organize a craft room so that everything is accessible and easy to use:

- Many crafts require a flat surface on which to work. Do yourself a favor and glue a wooden ruler or yardstick on one side of that flat surface. Crafters often need to measure things and this puts a measuring device right at your fingertips. Do not put it on the edge of the table where you work because sometimes you will need a flat edge. Instead, fasten it to a side or the back edge. It will double as a barrier to prevent items from falling off the table.

- Keep a basket or box for old newspapers, so they will be handy when you need to protect a work surface. If you frequently need this protection, stock up on cheap plastic tablecloths; you can keep them folded in a nearby basket for when they're needed.

- Put a rod in a closet, under a desk hutch, or across a narrow wall to hold ribbon, duct tape, masking tape, or other craft items you refer to frequently that come in rolls.

- Place magnetic strips on the wall to hold scissors and other tools that are metal.

- Put a bulletin board or dry erase paper in your craft room so you can plan and schedule out the priority level of your crafts. This can also be a handy place to write down things you need to buy. Better yet, put a pad of large sticky notes on your white board, along with a pen. That way you can jot down what you need and pull off the sheet to take your list with you when you go shopping. Bulletin boards are also very useful for sticking up pictures and notes of project ideas.

- If you do more than one type of craft – and you have the space available - it is helpful to divide your craft room into workstations for each craft. If you knit, stash your yarn and needles in one part of the room. If you make jewelry, store your jewelry tools and equipment in another area.

- Store fabric on individual hangers and hang them in a closet. I especially like the trouser hangers that have multiple bars. This way, you can see at a glance what fabrics you have available.

- Keep your yarn organized by color. Put all the reds together and all the blues in another clump. This makes it much easier to find what you want.

- Some metal tins are just tall enough to hold paint bottles and glue erect.

- Label, label, label, so you can find things fast.

Finding Supplies

Of course, your local craft store is the best option to procure craft supplies quickly. It's also a wonderful place to meet other crafters and exchange ideas and tips. Craft stores can be found all over the world, so there's probably one near you.

Wherever you are, you are likely to find a source of crafting supplies you can use for any number of projects. One recent development is the repurposing of trash. There's an entire art movement that uses found objects to create beautiful, often functional, works of art.

You can also purchase craft supplies online. Just perform an online search for your specific craft and you will find plenty of sites where you can purchase anything you need.

The Crafts

Now it's time to turn our attention to specific crafts. Each chapter that follows will detail a different kind of craft. You'll discover tips and tricks along with straightforward instructions you can follow to make each one.

Feel free to experiment. You can easily try a few crafts from each chapter, to get the big picture of what's out there. Then you can zero in on the crafts that are most interesting to you or that would make great gifts for specific friends. If you have an entrepreneurial bent, you can even sell your work online. Let's get started, shall we?

Chapter 2: Fabric Crafts

Working with fabric does not necessarily mean you have to know how to sew. It helps, but is not necessary. A few of the crafts in this chapter do require some sewing skill but many do not. Here's the trick: fabric is easily glued. Fabric glue will hold some seams together and can attach ornaments to fabric. Only when the craft is wearable or is designed for heavy-duty use will some form of sewing be necessary.

Drawstring Bag

The simple but versatile drawstring bag

A drawstring bag is useful for many things. Make one just big enough for your knitting projects or one that your wallet and brush will fit in. Make a bigger one for your notebook too. You can craft drawstring bags out of any type of fabric. I like little ones made of silk or satin, but I have made larger bags out of upholstery and other heavy materials.

You will need:

- Fabric.

- Pins.

- Ruler.

- Sewing machine.

- Needle and thread.

- Safety pin.

- Ribbon or string.

Cut two squares from the fabric. Make them any size you want. Place the fabric with right sides together and pin around three sides. Sew with a quarter-seam allowance starting three quarters of an inch from the top (the side you are not sewing) and go all the way around the bottom and up the other side, stopping when you have three quarters of an inch more fabric at the top edge. Clip the corners if the seams pucker, then iron them apart. The two places that have not been sewn at the top of each side need to be tacked down, so fold them inside to match with the seam allowance and hand sew with a running stitch so the top sides do not flair out. Fold the top down a quarter inch so that the right side is showing in a strip at the top. Iron this fold flat. Fold down another a half inch to make the casing. Pin and run a machine stitch very close to the edge so that you catch both layers. Finish it off and turn the bag right side out.

Attach a safety pin to the ribbon or string and work it through one side of the casing to the other, leaving enough to tie into a loop once you tighten the bag. This is the handle for the drawstring bag.

Fabric Bookmark

These little strips of stiff fabric make the best bookmarks ever and they are pretty, too. You can embellish them with ribbon, lace, or flat buttons if you like. As gifts you can customize them to reflect the personality or reading preferences of your recipients.

You will need:

- Thin fabric like cotton or muslin.

- Iron-on interfacing.

- Scissors.

- Pins.

- 1/2 inch ribbon.

- Thread.

- Sewing machine or needle.

- 1/8 to 1/2 inch ribbon.

- Pinking shears.

Cut two strips of fabric one inch wide and six inches long. Cut one piece of interfacing three-quarters of an inch by five and three-quarter inches. Iron on the fusible interfacing to the wrong side of one of the strips. Place the piece, interfacing up, on a table. Cut an eight-inch strip of ribbon and place it down the middle of the piece so that it hangs up over the top and the bottom. Lay the other fabric strip on top of this, with the right side facing out.

Pin around the edges. Sew a quarter-inch from the edge completely around the fabric strip, catching the ribbon in your stitches. Trim the edges of your bookmark with pinking shears to prevent the fabric from fraying.

Fabric-Covered Bins

Use small shoebox-sized bins on your first try. It can be a challenge to persuade the fabric to lay flat, so working on a smaller scale first will give you the skills you need to be able to tackle larger containers with ease.

You will need:

- Bins with matching lids.

- Tape measure.

- Fabric.

- Iron and ironing board.

- Needle and coordinating thread.

- Mod Podge.

- Paintbrush.

The lip of the bin is not covered with fabric so that it can snap shut and the bottom is also not covered. However, the fabric does fold under the bin about one and a half inches, so the top and bottom will look finished.

Measure from the lip of the bin to the bottom and cut strips of fabric to match the sides of your bin, allowing one extra inch at top and at bottom. You can cut your fabric lengthwise or sideways as you wish, just be consistent for all your pieces. Fold down a half inch of fabric and iron it. Do this for all sides of each fabric piece. This will prevent cut edges from fraying and will hide the selvage.

Spread Mod Podge on one side of the bin, covering the space where one strip of fabric will fit. Start directly beneath the lip of the container, laying the fabric over the Mod Podge and sticking it to the bin all the way to the bottom. There should be a one-inch excess of fabric at the bottom; leave it alone for now.

Attach your fabric to all sides of the bin, overlapping the edges slightly. Once the sides are dry, flip the bin upside down and Mod Podge the edges over the bottom. Let it dry. Make sure to push out any air bubbles by smoothing the fabric while you are applying it.

You can cover the lid with fabric, too, if you wish, or you can leave it plain. You also have the option of embellishing your bin with ribbon, beads, or silk flowers.

Fabric-Covered Bulletin Board

Plain old cork on a bulletin board is boring. Liven it up by covering it with fabric!

You will need:

- Bulletin board.

- Fabric.

- Tacky glue.

- Scissors.

- Ribbon.

Cut fabric to fit inside the borders of the bulletin board with three quarters of an inch extra on all sides. Fold down and iron a three-quarter-inch border all around, folding the edge of the fabric over the back. Run a fine line of glue along the top edge of the bulletin board near the border. Glue the fabric right side out, fitting the edge atop the glue at the top border. Run glue along each side and the bottom, doing the same.

You can decorate the edges with ribbon or make a crisscross pattern with the ribbon over the entire board by gluing down some ribbon.

Fabric-Covered Lampshade

A fabric-covered lampshade can add depth and warmth to a room. Most of the time, lampshades come in shades of white to beige, but you can make one any color or pattern you like with fabric.

You will need:

- Lampshade that is flat, with no ornamentation or pleats.

- Fabric.

- Iron and ironing board.

- Spray adhesive.

- Scissors.

- Tacky glue.

- Ribbon (optional).

Remove any trim from the lampshade so it is flat on all sides. Cut the fabric to fit, allowing three inches of extra width side to side and three quarters of an inch extra on the top and bottom. If you have a 12-inch diameter lampshade that is 12 inches tall, you would cut the fabric 15 inches side to side and 13 1/2 inches up and down.

Fold the top three quarter inch of fabric under and iron it flat. Do the same with the bottom. Iron down the three-inch margin on the side. Glue these areas with tacky glue.

Spray adhesive on the lampshade in sections and lay the strips right side out, with the top edge against the top, smoothing the fabric down toward the bottom. Keep the fabric as straight as possible, and work out any bubbles as soon as they appear. Fold the extra three inches onto the back of the lampshade, spray that strip with adhesive, and stick it to the lampshade. Slightly overlap the edge and reinforce this with tacky glue. Trim the top and bottom edges of the lampshade with ribbon, affixed with tacky glue, if you desire.

Fabric-Covered Notebook

Kids will love these fabric-covered notebooks to use at school or as journals. Adults like them, too.

You will need:

- Spiral notebook.

- Fabric.

- Pencil or marker.

- Ruler.

- Scissors.

- Tacky glue.

- Lightweight cardboard or poster board.

- Embellishments.

Spread the fabric, wrong side up, on a flat surface and lay the open notebook, on top. Make sure the notebook is straight along the grain of the fabric, then draw all around it with a pencil or light marker. Use a ruler to mark a two-inch border outside of the notebook. Cut along this outer edge. Fold the fabric over the edges of the notebook, gluing it down to the inside of the notebook. Keep the fabric taut. Cut a slit where the binding or spiral is on each side.

Cut two pieces of cardboard or poster board one inch smaller than the front and back covers. Do the same with fabric with and glue this to the cardboard, wrapping the edges over the back and gluing it down well. Place these pieces over the inside covers to hide the unfinished areas. Let them dry. You can embellish the outside of your notebook with ribbon, trim, or buttons, as you wish.

Fabric Headband

Easy-to-make headband adds style to your appearance.

The elastic at the back of this headband makes it easy to put on and keeps it in place.

You will need:

- One 14 by 11 inch strip of fabric.

- One seven-inch piece of three-quarter to one-inch-wide elastic.

- Thread and needle.

- Scissors.

- Iron and ironing board.

Cut the strip and the elastic. Cut another strip 14 inches wide by eight inches long for the elastic. You will be making a casing for the elastic. Fold both strips in half lengthwise, with the wrong sides together, and then sew along the long edge, giving a quarter-inch seam allowance. Turn right side out. Take one strip and insert the elastic, sending it all the way through. Tack to the short edge with needle and thread so it does not move. The fabric should crinkle up a bit. Flatten the other piece and press it. Pin the ends of the plain piece and the elastic piece together, and hand sew them. Clip threads and wear.

Fabric Heating Pad

This heating pad can be warmed in the microwave for a minute before placing it on an aching muscle. You can use these pads over and over again, so they make great gifts.

You will need:

- Soft fabric with no metallic enhancements. Fleece works best.

- Scissors.

- Thread.

- Pins.

- Sewing machine.

- Dry white rice (regular, not instant).

- Funnel.

Cut two seven-by-11-inch rectangles out of the fabric. If you're feeling whimsical, you can cut out animal shapes. If you want to target the neck, make your rectangle long enough to fit around a neck but slightly narrower.

Place one piece of the fabric right side up on a flat surface. Lay the other piece right side down on top and pin the edges together. Sew a quarter inch seam around the edge of the fabric, leaving four inches open on one side. Turn the piece right side out. Using a funnel, fill the fabric half to three fourths full of rice. Sew the opening shut and clip the loose threads.

Fabric Keychain

Most fabric stores have massive amounts of pretty trim and braid used to enhance clothing. These colorful strips of fabric, sometimes beaded, make beautiful keychains.

You will need:

- 10 inches of trim or braid.

- Needle and thread.

- Key chain ring.

Hold the trim with the wrong side up and fold one end up a half inch so the right side of the fold is up. Sew along the edge with a running stitch. Do the same on the other side. Turn the fabric so the right side is out, then fold the strip in half. Insert the ring between the two ends so that one end of the ring is between the fabric and the other end is hanging out below the fabric. Sew the trim together near the edge, catching the ring. Make sure the ring can move freely so you can attach keys.

Fabric Scrunchie

The versatile fabric scrunchie adds class to any outfit.

Add some class to your ponytail with a fabric scrunchie. They are very easy to make and accommodate almost any fabric. I recommend cotton, calicos, or silk. This craft is easy enough to make that you can easily coordinate your scrunchies with your wardrobe.

You will need:

- Small pieces of fabric.

- 3/8-inch-wide elastic.

- Sewing machine and thread.

- Safety pins.

- Needle.

- Pins.

Cut the fabric three by one inch for a child and four by 16 inches for an adult scrunchie. Cut elastic five inches long for a child and seven inches long for an adult.

Fold the fabric in half lengthwise, with the right sides facing. Pin them together near the edge. Machine sew this, making a half-inch seam but leaving the two ends open. Turn the scrunchie right side out.

Attach a safety pin to the end of the elastic and pin it to one end of the scrunchie. This will prevent the elastic from coming all the way through. Attach another safety pin to the other end of the elastic and thread it through the scrunchie and out the other end. Place the two ends of the elastic together and hand-sew them together with a running stitch. Let go of the elastic and it should pop inside the scrunchie. Now fold the ends of the fabric over just a little to make a hem and whip stitch the openings closed. Make sure the raw edges of the fabric are not showing.

Fabric-Covered Switch Plate

Use fabric to match your switches and outlet covers to your walls and your décor.

Switch plates are boring. You can spice them up by using fabric.

You will need:

- Fabric.

- Switch plate.

- Pencil or marker.

- Double-sided tape.

- Craft knife and scissors.

- Masking tape.

- Mod Podge.

- Paintbrush.

If you are using an existing switch plate, wash it well and let it dry completely. Place your fabric, face side down, on a work surface. Set the switch plate on top, trace around the outside edges with the pencil and then in the little rectangle where the switch goes. Make marks were the holes are for screws that hold the switch plate on the wall. Use a craft knife or scissors to cut an "X" in the center of the little rectangle for the switch and poke holes in the areas where the screw holes are. Don't worry about the fabric fraying because it will be covered with Mod Podge, which will prevent further unraveling. Cut around the traced edges, leaving a three-quarter-inch border around the switch plate. Cut the corner borders at a 45-degree angle.

Place a strip of double-sided tape around the four edges of the switch plate on the front. Match the holes and stick the fabric onto the front of the switch plate. The tape will hold it in place while you are working. Flip the plate over. Fold the fabric seam allowance over the edge of the switch plate and onto the back. Glue around the edges to secure the fabric to the back. Fold back the cuts you made at the switch hole onto the back of the plate and glue them in place. Use some masking tape to secure the back until it dries. This should be removed later.

Brush Mod Podge over the entire front of the switch plate. Let it dry and then give it another coat. Let this coat dry before you install your fancy new switch plate on the wall.

Felt Animals

Stuffed felt animals can be as elaborate as you want or as simple as this small chick.

35

Kids and cats love these animals and you can make them as big or small as you like. I use cookie cutters as a pattern, but when making larger animals I just draw them freehand.

You will need:

- Felt.

- Pins.

- Embroidery thread and needles.

- Buttons, ribbon other embellishments (don't use for babies).

- Polyester fiberfill.

Cut out two of the same animal shape from the felt. Sew on any embellishments to the front piece like embroidery or button eyes, embroidered features and more. Set pieces with wrong sides together and pin together. I use a whip stitch all around the animal but you can also sew with a quarter-seam allowance all around. Just leave about three to four inches open at the bottom or side. You can also pin it together with the wrong sides out and sew it on a machine, then turn right side out through the hole.

Fill with polyester fiberfill and whipstitch the opening shut.

You can easily make dinosaurs, cats, dogs, elephants, giraffes, and other animals. You are only limited by your imagination.

Felt Coasters

These coasters are colorful and pretty.

You will need:

- Felt in any color.

- Adhesive-backed felt in coordinating colors.

- Ruler.

- Pencil.

There are several ways you can make these coasters. The adhesive-backed felt is the visible part of the coaster and the felt part will lie against the table. Cut one four-inch square out of the adhesive-backed felt. You can cut another four-inch square from the regular felt and cut a star or heart from more of the adhesive backed felt. Remove the protective paper from the four-inch square, stick the regular four-inch square over the top, remove the protective paper from the shape, and stick it on the regular felt.

Another method is to cut four squares of regular felt that will fit in the 4-inch square and stick them on like a patchwork quilt.

Felt Heart Ornaments

Felt Heart

Hang these on lamp switches or on cupboard handles to add a little whimsy.

You will need:

- Felt squares (red, pink, purple, or white).

- Coordinating embroidery thread split into single strands.

- Tacky glue.

- Embroidery needle.

- Polyester fiberfill.

Cut two hearts from the felt. Separate the strands of embroidery thread, cut a four-inch piece, and tie it in a loop. Glue this loop to the inside of one heart with the knot down inside the heart about one inch, between the two humps.

Thread the needle with one strand of embroidery thread. Make a knot in the end and insert the thread at the point of the heart so that the knot is on the inside of the heart. Starting at that spot, sew the two hearts together, using a whip stitch. Stop when you have only a one-inch opening left and let the thread just hang for the moment. Stuff the heart with fiberfill. Do not overstuff or you'll find it very difficult to sew the heart shut. Once the heart is full, sew the gap closed. Make a knot and cut off the rest of the thread.

You can bead – or otherwise ornament – the front of the hearts before you sew them together if you want. You can also sew on ribbons or bows to further adorn your heart ornament.

Felt Play Mat

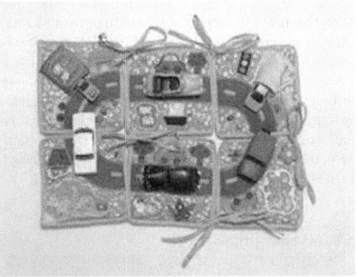

Modular Play Mat With Tie-Together Strings

This mat will show neighborhood landmarks and streets that kids can drive their matchbox cars along.

You will need:

- 1 yard green felt.

- 1/2 yard black or gray felt.

- 1/2 yard yellow felt.

- Felt squares to make buildings with.

- Scissors.

- Tacky Glue.

If you desire, get the adhesive-backed felt and just stick the shapes onto the green felt. Otherwise, you'll use tacky glue to adhere the streets and buildings to the green felt.

Adhesive-backed felt will not bend, so you won't be able to fold the mat up easily; if you do fold it, the shapes may fall off. It is better to sew your felt ornaments on the mat with running stitches rather than to glue them at all. They will stay on and you will be able to fold the mat when it is not in use.

Cut roads out of the black or gray felt and stick it on the green felt mat. Cut out thin rectangles from the yellow felt and put it down middle of the road for passing lanes. Make the roads wide enough for little cars. For buildings, include your house, a friend's house, the library, grandma's house, the grocery store, the gas station, school, and/or church, attaching them to the mat. You can also add farms out near the edges of the mat.

Framed Wall Hanging

Fabric can be an art form.

To make a thinner wall hanging use foam forms that will fit into a frame. Some of these forms have an adhesive front so you can just stick the fabric over the top. Make these the same way as the previous project, but use glue on the fourth side, instead of pins.

Hot Pad

Fabric potholders make great gifts.

This pattern makes a set of two hot pads from fabric.

You will need:

- 1/4 yard each of two different fabrics.

- 1/6 yard of binding edging.

- 1/4 yard insulated batting.

- nine-by-nine-inch pieces of cotton quilt batting.

- Needle and thread or sewing machine.

- Iron and ironing board.

Cut two 8-1/2 inch squares from one fabric and two more from the other fabric, giving you a total of four squares. Cut two nine-inch squares from the cotton batting and two more using the insulated batting.

To make one hot pad, lay face down on a table one fabric square. On top of that, layer an insulated batting square, a cotton batting square, and a fabric square from the coordinating fabric, this one facing up. Pin all the layers together.

Quilt the layers in cross hatch fashion with a sewing machine to make diamond shapes across the square. Trim all edges evenly.

With some binding fabric, cut a strip two and a half inches wide by six to eight inches more than length it takes to get around all the edges of the hot pad. Fold the binding strip in half with the wrong sides together and press with an iron. Unfold and turn down quarter-inch of the edge from front to the back of the binding and sew down to make a hem. Do the same on the other side.

Fold the binding strip over edge and pin it to the hot pad. Starting at one corner, sew as close to edge attached to binding strip as possible, making sure to catch both sides. When you reach a corner, fold to the right perpendicular to the seam and then fold back on itself to the left so you get a square edge, then sew it down. On the fourth side of your hot pad, use a needle and thread to connect the binding strip together. Press the finished product flat, then repeat the process to create the second hot pad.

No-Sew Accent Pillow

Stitch Witchery is a great product for those who do not sew but like to work with fabric. It comes in strips that you can cut to fit your needs. You literally glue your fabric pieces together by ironing Stitch Witchery strips between them.

You will need:

- Fabric.

- Stitch Witchery, one inch wide.

- Scissors.

- Pillow form.

- Iron.

- Needle and coordinating-colored thread.

Cut two pieces of fabric three inches larger than your pillow form. For example, if your pillow is 10 inches square you would cut two 13-inch-square pieces of fabric. Take one piece of fabric and fold a half inch over, ironing a seam. Do the same with the other piece of fabric.

Cut strips of Stitch Witchery to match the length of three sides of the pillow form. Place one piece of the fabric wrong side up and, starting with one side, slide the tape under the fold you just made. A half inch should stick out from the bottom. Do the same on the two other sides. Carefully iron only over the fabric; do not touch the iron directly to the stitch witchery itself. Do the same with the other piece of fabric.

Place the pieces together, wrong sides together, with the right side facing out. Make sure they match perfectly and use pins if you want to make sure they stay together. Iron over the edges to fuse the pieces together.

Place the pillow form through the open end and into the pillow. Use your needle and thread in a running stitch to secure this end of the pillow about a quarter inch from the edge. Keep your stitches even and sew through both thicknesses of the fabric. Continue your running stitch around the other three edges of the pillow as reinforcement.

No-Sew Blankets

Detail Of Tying No-Sew Blanket

This is the simplest way in the world to make a blanket. You can make these any size you want; you can size it for a crib, a couch cover up, or for a king sized bed. Fleece is sold in 60-inch wide bolts, but you can make the blanket as long as you want. Keep in mind when you're determining your size, that because you cut and tie the edges together, the blanket will be about 10 inches smaller than your initial fabric size.

You will need:

- Fleece material, two different colors (one a print, one a solid).

- Scissors.

- 5 by 5 inch piece of cardboard.

- Yardstick.

Cut one piece of fleece from the solid-color fabric and another of the same size from the printed fabric. Lay the pieces together and trim the two until they match exactly. Lay the five by five inch cardboard square in each corner and cut out the fabric around that template, discarding the fabric squares.

Lay a yardstick across one side, five inches up from the edge of the fabric. This will serve as your guide. You will create a fringe by cutting up to the ruler, through both layers of fabric. Your cuts will be about one inch apart Repeat this process for each side of the fabric.

Grasp one strip from the upper fleece layer and from its matching counterpart on the bottom. Tie the two fabric strips together in a double knot. Repeat this process all the way around. When you have tied each pair of fabric strips together, you will have a soft, snuggly blanket on your hands. Go ahead and cuddle up under its cozy warmth.

Oven Mitts

Make your oven mitts to fit your hands.

Use terrycloth or thick fleece for this project.

You will need:

- Newspaper.

- Pen or pencil.

- Ruler.

- Heavy fabric.

- Scissors.

- Pins.

- Sewing machine and thread.

Lay newspaper on a flat surface and set your palm flat on top of it. Trace around your hand, with your thumb sticking out to the side and then drawing a mitt around all your fingers together. Using a ruler, draw another line one inch outside of the first line, all the way around. This will be your cutting line. Go ahead and cut this out. Using it as a pattern, pin it to a double layer of fabric and cut it out; this will yield two mitt pieces.

Thread your sewing machine with matching or contrasting thread and stitch cross-hatches across each piece of fabric to create large diamonds throughout. Fold the bottom of each mitt a quarter-inch so that there is a quarter-inch strip of the right side folded to the wrong side. Stitch on machine, flip it over again, pin, then stitch one more time. This hems the bottom of the oven mitt.

Pin the two pieces of the mitt together with the wrong side out. Start at the edge of the thumb side and sew all around, with a quarter-inch seam allowance. Turn the mitt right side out.

Pillowcase

Make these pillowcases out of a soft cotton fabric. You can add lace edging to give your bedroom a touch of character, if you want.

You will need:

- Fabric.

- Scissors.

- Ruler.

- Pins.

- Lace or ribbon trim (optional).

- Sewing machine and thread.

- Needle and thread (optional).

Cut two pieces of fabric, 23 inches long by 31 inches wide. Place one piece on top the other with right sides of the fabric facing together. Sew three of the four sides together, leaving one of the short sides open with a quarter-inch seam allowance. Fold the unsewn edge toward you by a quarter inch and press it with an iron until it stays down. Fold the open fabric down again by three inches and pin it in place. Sew all the way around near the edge catching all thicknesses to make a wide hem.

You can leave the pillowcase like this. Just turn it right side out and use it to cover your pillow. If you want to add lace or edging, hand-stitch this onto the hem side. A regular pillow is 20 by 26 inches, so a normal pillow will fit it nicely. For queen or king-sized pillows, measure their dimensions and adjust your fabric dimensions to accommodate the larger size.

Tablecloth

You will need:

- Fabric – I recommend selecting a medium-weight, wrinkle-resistant fabric that does not stain easily.

- Iron and ironing board.

- Sewing machine and coordinating-colored thread.

The most important thing about making a tablecloth is size: you want enough fabric not only to cover the tabletop but also to gracefully drape over the edge by about one foot.

I have a three- by four-foot rectangular table. If I want to create a tablecloth for this particular table, I'll need a piece of fabric that will allow for a finished size of five by six feet. Keep in mind that you'll be taking half-inch seams around the edges, so you'll want to allow for that extra length on all four sides. Depending on the width of your fabric, you may find it necessary to create a seam across your tablecloth, sewing two pieces together to make it large enough.

After measuring and cutting your tablecloth to the proper rough size, place the fabric wrong-side up on a flat surface. Turn up a quarter-inch fold all around, pinning and ironing it flat. Fold this edge under again by another quarter inch, and iron it flat. Using a sewing machine, stitch through both layers of fabric to create a flat hem.

Quilt Block Wall Hanging

Sample Quilt Block

You can hand sew a plastic ring onto the center back of a quilt block to catch a nail and hang it on the wall, or you can create fabric strip loops that you sew between the front and back layers on either side of the top, then slip a dowel rod over them. You can also tie a piece of yarn to each side and hang it from that.

You will create a patchwork quilt block by cutting four squares that serve as backing squares, then sewing them together. You will then create top squares and appliqué a figure on the front.

You will need:

- Pins.

- Thread.

- Needles.

- Fabric for back, tip and any ornamentation.

- Quilt batting.

- One-inch wide seam binding.

Always wash your fabric *before* cutting, so that any shrinkage occurs at the very start of the process, not after you've pieced the parts together. Choose a quilt pattern and cut out all the pieces and backing square. Sew pieces for the front of the quilt square together per pattern and set aside.

Place the backing piece wrong side up on a flat surface. Cut a piece of batting about a quarter inch less on each side than the backing piece. If you are making a 1 by 12-inch square, the front and back piece is 1inches square, but the batting is a quarter-inch less on all sides (an 11 and three-quarter inch square). Center the batting on top of a backing piece and lay the front on top. Using a needle and contrasting thread, baste the three layers together. Sew the square together using a quarter-inch seam allowance, even though you really aren't making a seam. Either hand- or machine-quilt your quilt block as desired.

Take one-inch-wide seam binding and pin it to the edge of the quilt block, starting at a bottom corner. Pin it over the edges to the front and back, squaring the corners. Sew the binding tape to the quilt square, as closely to the edge that connects with the quilt block as possible.

Sleep Pillow

Sleep pillows are filled with scented potpourri and fit inside a regular pillow. When filled with the correct herbs, they induce sleep. You can use chamomile, hops, lavender, and rose petals, along with a fixative and a few drops of corresponding essential oils. When you fill the sleep pillow, make sure it lies flat so it isn't too bulky and uncomfortable to lay your head upon.

You will need:

- 6-inch squares of loosely woven fabric (cotton or muslin works well).

- Pins.

- Thread and needle or sewing machine.

- Iron and Ironing board.

- Potpourri.

- Funnel.

- Ribbon.

- 1/4 inch ribbon.

- Scissors.

Pin the squares together with the right sides facing. Sew three sides, using a half-inch seam allowance. Fold down the raw edge one eighth of an inch from the unsewn edge and press it flat. Fold another three quarters of an inch down and stitch close to where the edge meets the body of the pillow to make a casing. Put a safety pin in the end of the ribbon and thread it through the casing. Cut the ribbon long enough so you can draw the sleep pillow closed and tie it off so that nothing falls out.

Fill the pillow with potpourri and tie it closed. Insert into a pillow with the pillowcase on at the top so your head rests against it.

Sunglasses Case

Felt sunglasses protectors are easily fashioned and make great gifts.

I like to use either felt or fleece for this project because neither one frays and you don't have to worry about hemming.

You will need:

- Fabric.

- Scissors.

- Sewing machine and thread.

- Fusible interfacing.

- Iron and ironing board.

- Embroidery thread and needle.

Cut four pieces of fabric into seven and a half by four and a half inch rectangles. Cut two of the same size pieces from fusible interfacing. Iron the interfacing to the wrong sides of two of the pieces of fabric. Place the plain piece of fabric on top, then the interfacing piece, right side out, and pin together. Run a stitch around each pair of pieces, so that the interfacing is enclosed like a sandwich.

Before you sew everything together, you'll want to consider what decorations – if any – you want to use. You can sew on ribbon or beads; you can embroider your initials or embellish the case with embroidered flowers if you prefer. You can use appliqué or fabric paint...the sky's the limit. Whatever you choose, you'll want to apply your decorations before you proceed with sewing the case together.

Now that you've decorated the outside, pin the pieces together. Hand sew the two long sides and one short side together using a whip stitch. You'll keep one side open in which to slide the sunglasses. Start at the opening and sew down one long side to the short side and back up the other long side.

Insert your glasses, and you're ready to go.

Wall Hangings

Fabric can provide a dramatic focal point.

Many fabrics are gorgeous enough to be viewed as art objects all by themselves. 'That's where wall hangings come in. You can make thick wall hangings, with quilting to accentuate the details. You can also frame a beautiful fabric. Read on.

You will need:

- Fabric.

- Styrofoam or foam forms.

- Pins.

- Glue or spray adhesive.

- A bar to hang your project from.

Use a sheet of half-inch to two-inch thick Styrofoam to make a wall hanging that does not require a frame. Place the Styrofoam against the wrong side of the fabric and cut the fabric around it, giving an extra three to five inches seam allowance. Fold the fabric over the Styrofoam, as if you are wrapping a present. Use pins near the top to hold the fabric taut at the edge on the back side.

Do not use hot glue to secure the fabric in place because it will melt the Styrofoam. Instead, use tacky glue or a glue without solvent, so you can avoid dissolving the Styrofoam backing. You can also use duct tape on fabric for a firm hold. 3M makes a glue that will stick to Styrofoam called Super 77. Spray adhesive will also work. Use glue to attach a bar to the top back of the project. After the glue is dry, you can hang your project wherever you like.

Chapter 3: Scrapbooking

Scrapbooking is very popular and it is the best way to preserve memories from the past in an organized and appealing manner. The crafts below will give you ideas for many different types of scrapbooks. Throughout the other chapters of this book, you will find scrapbook paper employed in unique ways. I use it for jewelry making and in holiday crafts. The paper is so pretty, you will want to use it everywhere, from insets on your cupboard doors to coasters.

Scrapbooks most often appear in two popular sizes, 12 by 12 inches and 8.5 by 11 inches. But, why limit yourself to the traditional? This is *your* scrapbook, so choose a size that appeals to you! You can go as small as a mini-scrapbook at four by four inches.

Scrapbook Page Design

Here are some tips to follow when creating a scrapbook:

- **Choose a focal point on each page**. Arrange everything else on the page around this focal point. If you are creating a scrapbook on your trip to Niagara Falls, you may choose a general picture of the falls to be the primary focal point. You would then arrange other things around this picture that pertain to the subject: tickets to one of the attractions at the falls, brochures, pictures of riding the Maid of the Mist, or photos of the family at the gardens on the Canadian side.

- Keep in mind you don't have to keep your photos the same size; you can trim or crop them as you see fit to help fit them best in your design. Digital pictures are easy to resize and even recolor to fit in with your general design theme. Then you can print them out with a photo printer. I have quite a few incredible poster size collages of my favorite images on my office wall right now. I got them professionally framed. All original design. I love them and I have had a lot of positive reactions to them from people who have seen them over the years.

- Use the right supplies. You will need acid-free card stock, scrapbook and papers, durable colored pens, along with acid-free adhesives, things to embellish your display, a paper trimmer, scissors, photos, and page protectors. Always use acid free adhesives, whether tape or liquid. This will preserve your scrapbook in good shape for years to come and will protect the photos from discoloration.

- Keep it simple – you don't have to use all your photos. Store most of them elsewhere, selecting the three or four that best tell your story or reinforce the theme of the page.

- Caption your photos. You won't always remember the details (trust me, I know from experience) and other people won't know the backstory behind a specific photo unless you tell them. Your brief descriptions will make your scrapbook both intelligible and interesting for decades to come.

- Don't use professional photos themselves in a scrapbook. It is better to preserve these photos elsewhere instead of cutting them up to put in a scrapbook. You can easily make copies of these professional photos and crop them to your heart's content.

- Don't go overboard with embellishments. When you visit a craft store and see all the available embellishments, it is hard *not* to go overboard and buy them all, but you will want to use restraint when you lay out your pages. If the eye has too much to look at on a page, it will give up, and your viewers will miss the point of your page. Keep your embellishments to a tasteful minimum.

- Most scrapbooks come with just a few pages, but you can always buy more. Just remember that only a few will fit in the book as is. If you want a thicker book, you may need to purchase extenders, little metal rods that go through the holes in the book to hold it together and allow for more pages.

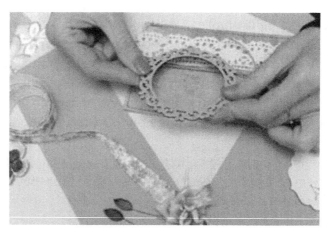
Scrapbooking Details

Theme-Based Scrapbooking

There are two basic ways to organize a scrapbook. Yours will naturally organize itself according to either themes or a largely chronological story line. For example, when I was a child I was crazy about horses, so I put together a theme-based scrapbook that contained everything I could get my hands on about horses.

Other examples of theme-based scrapbooks would include:

- Places I've Travelled.

- My Child's Sports.

- My Goals and How I Pursued Them.

- My Vacation.

- Friendships for Life.

- Pets in My Life.

- Cars I've Restored.

- My Gratitude Album.

- Concerts and Events I've Attended.

Almost anything that interests you can be turned into a theme-based scrapbook! You can turn theme-based scrapbooks into gifts that friends and family will cherish. Children will love a scrapbook of their favorite things. For younger children, a sturdy alphabet scrapbook using familiar images can prepare a child for reading. Older children will appreciate a scrapbook about their favorite activities. Friends will love a scrapbook celebrating your friendship or marking important events in their lives.

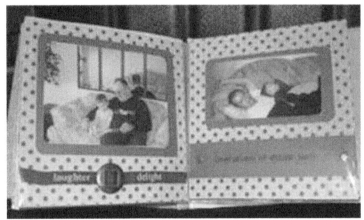

Laminate pages for baby's own scrapbook.

Art Scrapbook

Kids frequently bring artwork home from school and there's only so much space on the fridge for display, so why not preserve them in a scrapbook? If you like to sketch in your spare time, why not capture those scraps of paper in a place you can enjoy them?

Scrapbooks are a wonderful way to track the progression of your artistic interests and watch how your artistic voice develops over time. My aunt kept her son's best artwork, from the time he started drawing as a child on into his adult career as a professional artist. She has even been known to sneak into his New York City studio and take photos of finished projects. She put everything in a scrapbook she created; it provides a beautiful tracing of his artistic development; in it you can see similarities between the things he drew in kindergarten and what he is doing professionally now.

Baby Scrapbook

You can include in this scrapbook the hat the hospital gave your baby, along with the hospital bracelets both mom and baby wore and the crib marker or room marker.

Paint the baby's foot with a little nontoxic paint and press it against cardstock for a first footprint. If you want, you can use the same paint to create matching handprints.

You can include a copy of the birth certificate, vaccination records, christening announcements, and other items in this scrapbook, but always store the originals in a safe place. Of course, you'll want to include plenty of photos to commemorate your baby's first days and weeks, captioned with your precious memories.

Bucket List Scrapbook

This scrapbook is the perfect place to list everything you want to do before you die. I made one for my 18-year-old nephew when he graduated from high school and he has kept it up himself, ever since. When he accomplishes one of the items on his bucket list, he puts big gold star on the page. This is helping him to keep his dreams in mind as he goes through life.

Diary Scrapbook

Each week my cousin takes a scrapbook page and handwrites a diary, commemorating the events of the past seven days. She includes pictures, business cards she has collected, a pretty flower she picked, newspaper and magazine articles that caught her eye, bulletins from church with her notes marking those times a particular song or sermon touched her heart, and other things that impacted her life during the week. She now has several years' worth of scrapbooks; I suspect they'll be handed to hand down to her children one day.

Family Tree Scrapbook

Sample Family Tree Scrapbook Cover

The first page of this type of scrapbook is will be the traditional diagram of the actual family tree, with just names and dates. You can opt to print one from Ancestry.com or make your own tree with scrapbook paper and leaves with the names, followed by the birth and death dates of each individual.

The pages that follow will flesh out the story of their lives and the dynamics of their relationships. Of course, you'll want to include plenty of photos of family members. You can create pages honoring specific individuals, couples, or other significant relationships. You can include letters from family members, wedding invitations, or newspaper clippings, public announcements, and award certificates. Don't forget to provide the anecdotes that add character to your forbears; include your personal reminiscences as well as the recounted stories of multiple generations.

Favorite Quote Scrapbook

I love quotes. You can build a quote scrapbook by collecting your favorite quotes and adding illustrations or photos to them. One of my favorite quotes is from Maya Angelou, – "Try to be a rainbow in someone's cloud." I would print that quote on a page, then attach cloud-shaped quilt batting, out of which I would draw a multi-hued rainbow, using vivid oil pastels.

Foodie Scrapbook

Are you a foodie? If so, a foodie scrapbook is just what you need to preserve your recipes and keep your ideas flowing. You can include things like printed menus from a favorite restaurant, individual recipes with matching photos, illustrations or descriptions showing unique ways for presenting dishes., If you are a wine aficionado, include notable wine labels along with a description of the wine's characteristics, its history, and the special event that triggered its uncorking.

You can include successful menus from past parties, giving a brief reminder of what worked well. Include wrappers from favorite foods or and labels from cans of food that were hard to come by or are just amusing or memorable. Include anything that makes your foodie heart beat faster.

Gardening Scrapbook

My neighbor is a wonderful gardener; his wife always participates in the process by making an annual garden scrapbook each year. He finds this invaluable because he can look back and remember what has succeeded year after year and – more importantly – what should never be tried again, because it was a monumental flop! His wife's scrapbooks also remind him when he needs to rotate his crops to replenish the soil and they help him see which plants will do best in which specific locations.

Along with enticing photographs of the garden in all stages of life, my neighbor preserves soil test results, seed packages, newspaper and magazine clippings with new things to try, and journaling excerpts on what worked in his garden and what didn't.

My neighbor needs this ongoing record of his garden; you see, he's got quite an extensive garden space. He grows everything from apple trees to vegetables to flowers. You haven't lived until you go outside in the morning, look across the fence, and see umbrellas opening over his beautiful Dahlias to protect the blooms until he can enter them in the county fair. This man *knows* his garden, in large part thanks to the scrapbooking efforts of his wife.

Gift Scrapbook

My neighbor's kids are always asking her to make a list of what gifts she would like to receive for one holiday or another. Being an avid scrapbooker, she filled a mini scrapbook with things she would like to have. In some cases she went to a store and took photos; in others she cut pictures out of store fliers. Her scrapbook now contains all the stuff she would appreciate getting as a gift. It is, of course, embellished in true scrapbooker fashion with pretty scrapbook paper, ribbons, bows, flowers and other decorations. Her children are relieved to know exactly what to get their mother for her next birthday and she's glad to know she'll get something she can be excited about.

Goals Scrapbook

Everyone should have goals. Make a scrapbook that details your own. When you do reach them, add a scrapbook page that celebrates your success.

When your goals change, as they inevitably do, you can update your scrapbook pages to more appropriately represent them. In this way you will have both an encouraging historical record of your reached goals, and a motivational document to spur you on to reach the goals that are pending.

Holiday Scrapbook

My sister loves Halloween. She has created an elaborate a Halloween scrapbook that probably should be published, it's that good. She has included illustrations and explanations of the history of Halloween as a holiday, including a picture of her attempt to carve a turnip. (Did you know modern day jack-o-lanterns started out as turnips?). She has provided pictures of costumes along with their patterns. Her scrapbook includes interesting recipes of fun food for Halloween, like hot dog mummies and jack-o-lantern sandwiches. She has included descriptions and pictures of Halloween party games that beat bobbing for apples to smithereens!

If you have a favorite holiday, celebrate it by making a scrapbook!

Love Letter Scrapbook

I had a friend whose grandmother and grandfather wrote back and forth to each other while he was serving as a soldier in the Second World War. They both kept the letters. After he died, my friend was helping her mother prepare the house to for sale. She came upon both sets of letters, stashed in an old hatbox in the bedroom.

After arranging them in chronological order, she took the single sided letters and carefully affixed them to scrapbook pages. She preserved the double-sided letters in page protectors that she then attached to the scrapbook.

My friend also included old pictures of her grandparents from the timeframe of the letters. She then extended the pages to include memories from when they met, their wedding, and on through the birth of their children. She offered the finished product to her grandmother 10 years after her grandfather had died. It became a cherished possession that sparked many story sessions with the grandchildren. Now that grandma is gone, my friend has passed the scrapbook down to her children to keep the memories and stories alive for additional generations.

Medical Scrapbook

This scrapbook is the place to clearly indicate your medical conditions. You can include articles on each problem so that anyone who reads the scrapbook will be able to understand what you're dealing with. If you have diabetes, for example, you can include an article on how diabetes affects the body. You can add a clear description of what happens when you experience low or high blood sugar and explain how caregivers can identify and treat each symptom.

Use a page to detail your current medications. You can include a page to describe visits to the doctor and one to help you keep track of things you need to do to maintain your health. For example, you can include a page that indicates your exercise plan for each day and provides a place you can log your participation. For chronic ailments, you can include information on the latest developments in treatment and detail medical advances you wish were developed.

Nature Scrapbook

Perhaps you enjoy going hiking and want to create a scrapbook to record what you've seen and experienced. While hiking, collect flowers, grasses, leaves, feathers, small twigs, little stones, and other things that catch your eye. Take pictures with your phone of impressive landscapes, squirrels playing under a pine tree, or interesting rock formations.

Immediately upon your return, you'll want to record the location and the date these items were found. Jot down notes to remind you of what happened that day to give context to these items when you go to place them in your scrapbook.

Next, you'll want to press the flowers, leaves and grasses to dry them and make them flat enough to lay well on a scrapbook page. Place each item on an absorbent paper towel and lay it between the pages of a large book. An old dictionary or encyclopedia works well. Lay another piece of paper towel on top and close the book.

If you have items of varying thickness it's best to press them individually, between different pages of the book. You can press several items of similar thickness in a single location; just do not allow them to touch. Then, close the book, stack a few other heavy books on top, and forget about it for about three weeks.

After a few weeks have elapsed, open your book and remove the flattened items. They should be completely dry. You can use tweezers to gently position them on scrapbook paper atop a little glue, spread on thinly with a brush. Lightly press the items down onto the glue. These pressed items will be very delicate, so be careful.

You can incorporate thicker items, like twigs and stones, in your scrapbook by securing them in a 35-millimeter slide sleeve. You'll want to either staple or stitch the sleeve shut with embroidery thread and a heavy-duty needle before adding it to your scrapbook.

Party Scrapbook

Are you having a first birthday party for a grandchild or a sweet 16 party for a daughter? Birthdays, especially significant ones, are a rich source for scrapbooking. In addition to photos of the day, you can include samples of party hats, streamers, favors, and other artifacts that helped to make the day special.

Pet Scrapbook

Horse scrapbook cover

Pictures of your pet should go into a pet scrapbook, along with other items that evoke memories of your times together. An old collar can be stored in a slide sleeve. You can take a flat circle of polymer clay and press your pet's paw in it to make a paw print impression. After following the baking instructions for the clay and cooling it to room temperature, you can store your paw print in a slide sleeve as well.

You can easily and safely record your pet's paw prints by using non-toxic paint designed for finger painting and pressing the print onto acid-free paper. You might want to take this project outdoors on a driveway or sidewalk, to avoid Fido's prints on your carpet. When you're done, a swipe with a wet rag, a run across the lawn, or walking through a mud puddle should remove the paint.

You can include old pet registration tags in this scrapbook, old toys that aren't used anymore, or a scrap of that baby blanket your pet loved so much he reduced to shreds. It's also a good idea to store pet vaccination and other medical records in your scrapbook; this provides a safe and easily accessible storage space for this vital information, so you always know it is.

Positive Affirmation Scrapbook

Positive affirmations can be photographed, written, or painted on a scrapbook page.

A friend of mine has made an absolutely beautiful affirmation scrapbook; she takes it out and looks at it frequently in order to stay positive, even in her most difficult days.

My friend started by selecting several affirmations that are important to her. She wrote them down, each one on a separate scrapbook page, and added beautiful pictures that represent those affirmations. She either took the pictures herself or found them in magazines and clipped them out. Here is an example one of her pages:

The page reads, "I have as much brightness to offer the world as the next person." The scrapbook paper she used was full of tiny little light bulbs. She drew a cartoon image of a bright lightbulb and affixed it in the very center of the page.

Whenever my friend meditates, she grabs the book, finds an affirmation – like the lightbulb page – that applies to her in that moment; she opens the scrapbook to that page and concentrates on speaking that affirmation aloud several times while she focuses on the associated image.

Schooldays Scrapbook

Preserving your memories of your child's time in school can develop into a long-term scrapbooking project. Depending on how detailed you want to get, you can use a single large volume to preserve class photos and highlights of elementary school, or you may wish to record details of each grade in a separate volume.

You can portray the year from your child's point of view, captioning images with direct quotes by your offspring and using artifacts your child created or valued highly. If you prefer, you can build a scrapbook from a mother's perspective, recounting anecdotes that were special to you. Whatever approach you take – and there's nothing to prevent you from mixing perspectives – a schooldays scrapbook can keep those precious memories alive, both for yourself and for your child.

This kind of scrapbook can add depth to a graduation celebration. When you present it to your child, it can also serve as a rite of passage that marks the beginning of adulthood. In addition to formal class portraits, you can include pictures you've taken, friends' photos, images and posts from social media, important papers, artwork, report cards, news clippings, special items your child has collected, and anything that depicts your child's interests, friendships, and achievements.

Seashore Scrapbook

Preserve those sunny memories in a scrapbook!

Pick up some 35-millimeter slide sleeves for your seashore scrapbook. These sleeves have little compartments that you can glue, staple, or sew shut, allowing you to feature things like sand from the beach, pieces of driftwood, shells, beach stones, sea glass, and generally anything that would not otherwise fit into a scrapbook.

When it comes to shells, check to ensure that whatever was living in the shell before you picked it up is no longer living there. Nothing smells worse than a rotting shell and the stench can permeate your whole scrapbook! You'll want to wash them carefully and let them dry completely before you lay them out.

Of course, you'll want to include pictures of fun in the sun, captioning them so that you'll remember the smell of salt tang and the feel of the wind in your hair. Photos can capture the refreshing spirit of the beach, enabling you to feel the warm sun on your skin long after you return home.

Storytelling Scrapbooks

Whenever you wish to commemorate a series of events, you can think of it as telling a story. Your scrapbook will be largely chronological, although there's nothing wrong with inserting thematic-focused pages into the work.

A wedding scrapbook is an excellent example of storytelling format. You can follow the bride from the time she gets up in the morning through the last-minute preparations, getting dressed, traveling to the wedding venue, the ceremony, and the on through the events that occur during the reception. If you wish, you can weave together parallel threads of the groom's day as well, combining both viewpoints into one tale of their big day.

For a unique perspective, you could tell the story from the point of view of the flower girl or the ring bearer. As the mother of the bride, you can present a unique gift by weaving past and present into a scrapbook of reminiscences, wishes, and hopes for the new couple. You are telling the story of the wedding, but that story can take any number of forms.

A long-term story form of scrapbooking can provide a record of your child's school days, from an adult perspective. You can begin when your child enters school for the first time and carry your scrapbooking forward as your child progresses through school. Devote several pages to each year, including photos and artifacts that depict the highlights of each year in your child's life. Then, upon graduation from high school or college, you can present this gift to your child, celebrating all the small milestones that led up to graduation.

Thankfulness Scrapbook

If you ever need want to be reminded of all the things you are grateful for, start a thankfulness scrapbook. Whenever you get feel down and out, just pull it out the scrapbook and remind yourself of everyone and everything in your life that is praiseworthy, delightful, and worthwhile. It will raise your spirits beyond belief.

A thankfulness scrapbook needn't be a one-time static endeavor. Whenever a significant event occurs, add a page to your scrapbook. As you discover new sources of encouragement and refreshment, include them as well. In this way, a thankfulness scrapbook can serve you as an ongoing source of encouragement and a reminder of your spiritual richness.

To The Bride Scrapbook

Everyone has advice to for a new couple when they get married. A scrapbook is a wonderful place to record those bits and pieces. You have the option to create your scrapbook as a personal gift to the bride and groom or you can solicit advice from their friends and family. Either way, present the results to the bride at a wedding shower, along with a more practical gift. I'll bet the bride remembers the scrapbook longer than she remembers the gift.

This kind of scrapbook is highly versatile. It can include a section full of recipes that are easy, quick to make, and delicious. Another section might include helpful hints on how to make the house more comfortable. You can provide pages with activities that can help the couple deepen their relationship, along with ideas for things they can do spice up date night.

The sky is the limit here. Let You can even include a "Don't Do This" section, offering personal experiences that backfired, in hopes that the new couple will be able to avoid them, or at the very least, get a good laugh out of them!

Travel Scrapbook

A travel scrapbook cover from a trip to France

Here's where you can put the trinkets from your travel adventures, such as brochures, postcards, flowers, matchbooks, and business cards. To tell the story of your travels, include captioned photographs. One of my friends makes a new scrapbook for each vacation she takes. She will print out a map and outline the route they took with a highlighter; this will be her first page. She then fills the additional pages with whatever she collected while on that trip. She has included sand from various beaches in slide protectors along with driftwood samples and stones.

Whenever my friend travels, she carries along paper towels and a sturdy book in which to press leaves and flowers. She writes a detailed journal of each day and uses these notes to help her flesh out the memories of her travels when she compiles her travel scrapbook.

Wedding Scrapbook

Save an invitation along with an RSVP card to serve as the title page of your wedding scrapbook. Press individual flowers from the bouquets. You can also include printed napkins, programs from the wedding, and labels from wine bottles. You can set disposable cameras on the reception tables and ask guests to use them to take photos. You can also invite your friends to send you photos they have taken of the event; that way you'll have multiple perspectives of the event. Choose the best storytelling photos to include in your scrapbook.

Year-In-Review Scrapbook

Start your scrapbook with New Year's Day; jot down all your resolutions and goals for the year, then make pages for the rest of your year. You can include your predictions for your friends and family, noting, for example, if you anticipate a graduation or new baby to be born. Save this scrapbook until New Year's Eve. Then open the pages and see how closely the year matched your predictions.

Chapter 4: Painting Crafts

Painting is a popular craft because you can paint on just about anything; the most common media are glass, fabric, canvas, and wood, but pretty much anything that will hold still long enough can be painted.

Different projects require different types of paint. Art paints such as watercolors and oil paints are specific to certain media: watercolor paper for the first and canvas for latter. Acrylic paints, often dubbed "craft paints," work well on a wide range of surfaces. You'll find a whole array of acrylic paints formulated for specific media - concrete acrylics, glass acrylics, metal acrylics, and plastic acrylics: this last type is used on model cars and airplanes. Fabric paint is specifically designed to bond with cotton fibers. Spray paint has many uses in the world of crafts, as does air brushing.

Tips For Painting

The following are a few tips that will help you decide what kind of paint to use on a project:

- With fabric, only use fabric paint. You can sometimes use an acrylic craft paint, but it isn't formulated to last through repeated wash cycles.

- You can use screen printing paint on fabric; it does not bleed and creates nice clean lines. Simply Screen is a type of screen paint suitable for fabrics. Always wash your fabric before applying paint; you'll want to remove any fluff plus any chemical residue from the manufacturing process that could interfere with paint adherence.

- Glass is easily painted with acrylic and tempera paints, but it is covered much more effectively with model enamel. The paint used on model cars works quite nicely on glass, especially when you have detailed work and need to paint fine lines.

- Spray paint comes in a variety of finishes ranging from high gloss, to matte finish. It also comes in various mottled finishes. Wood will require a primer before using spray paint. Metal surfaces last longest when you use a use a rust-fighting spray paint. Remember, spray paint requires from 24 to 48 hours to dry completely.

- Painting on plastic can be a challenge because plastic bends, stretching the paint. However, you now can find paint designed specifically for use on plastic surfaces. Other options are to use model paint or to try automotive spray paint. In any case, priming is essential, to ensure a solid bond with the plastic medium.

- You can apply spray paint to wood, but for fine detail work it is better to use an acrylic paint. Other paints for use on wood are chalk paint and exterior or interior latex house paint.

Canvas Wall Hangings

Almost everyone could use a work of art to hang on their wall and enhance their environment. Here is a simple, never-fail project that will have your visitors oohing and aahing.

You will need:

- Canvas.

- Paint.

- Paintbrush or sponge.

- Stencils (optional).

- Leaves, sticks, other nature articles (optional).

- Painter's tape.

If you don't plan to frame your art, opt for the raised canvas that looks like a flattened box, or a framed flat canvas. Both types are pretty inexpensive. In either case, I suggest using the canvas that has already been treated with Gesso. Gesso whitens the canvas and seals it so the paint won't soak into the fibers and bleed or fade.

The first step is to create a background wash. Thin out some paint a bit and start brushing it on the canvas. Start painting at the area you want to have the strongest color and brush outward. This will enable you to create a gradient from dark to light. As you paint outward, add water to the paint (or linseed oil for oil-based paints) to further decrease the color saturation. When you have covered the entire canvas, let the surface dry completely before proceeding.

Here are several ways you can make a great painted canvas wall hanging without even knowing how to draw.

- Use letter stencils to print words across the canvas, painting them a solid color. You can also leave the letters the color of the background and paint a darker color outside of the letter shapes.

- Cut shapes out of painter's tape, stick them onto the dried canvas, and spray or splatter paint atop them. After the paint is completely dry, remove the painter's tape to reveal your shapes in the midst of the color.

- Flatten leaves, sticks, ferns, or other items from nature and attach them to the canvas, using a little painter's tape to hold them down. Spray or spatter paint over the surface area.

- You can also use leaves (or other natural items) as stamps. Paint the leaves themselves and carefully press them onto the dried canvas to mark it.

Dripped Canvas Wall Hanging

Detail of dripped paint on canvas

Here is another canvas wall-hanging project. In this case you'll want to use the raised, thick canvas.

You will need:

- Canvas, pre-stretched over a frame.

- Spray paint.

- Acrylic craft paint.

- Water.

- Squeeze bottles (like the ones for mustard and catsup bottles).

Spray paint the canvas, covering it completely in a solid color. Use any type of spray paint, from glossy finish to metallic. Let this dry thoroughly before you proceed.

Place the canvas on top of a floor that is protected from possible paint spatters, standing it at a steep angle against a similarly protected wall. Prepare three or four different colors of paint in individual squeeze bottles, diluting one to two tablespoons of paint with a quarter cup of water. You want the paint to be thin enough to drip down the canvas. Before each squirt, shake the bottles well. Squirt the lightest color along the top edge of the canvas, allowing it to drip down to the bottom.

You can let your first color dry before adding another or you can drizzle on the next color immediately, allowing them to mingle and blend. This can create some interesting effects. For example, if you drip apply yellow and then red, some of the drips will blend and mingle to produce orange. Just don't drip too much or everything will turn an ugly brown!

You can play with the canvas itself, turning it different directions. The drips will continue to sag downward, but "down" is now toward a different edge of the canvas. You can introduce new colors to a different side of the canvas, too.

Painted Accent Pillow

Before you complete your accent pillow in the fabric section of this book, you might want to paint the pillow cover first. Wash the fabric before sewing it and then use fabric paint to draw polka dots, squares, or freehand figures on it. Stencils are another option. Once everything dries, continue by stuffing the pillow with the pillow form and sewing it up to complete the pillow-making process.

Painted Apron

Purchase a muslin bib apron from your local craft store and go wild with fabric paint. Wash and dry it first, then iron the sucker smooth and start painting.

If you need an idea to get you going, you can start by painting red and white checkers across the top of the bib. Then, paint some big sunflowers in the middle. With fabric paints you are free to make almost anything your mind can imagine.

Painted Bird House

This ornamental bird house adds a warm touch to any home.

Wooden birdhouses come in all sizes and shapes; you can find them at a craft store. Most paintable bird houses are not for birds to live in, but exist to add interest to your yard or home. You can easily pick one up at your local craft store and paint it to enhance the décor of your kitchen or living room, or to grace a porch or garden.

You will need:

- Wooden birdhouse.

- Brush or paint sponge.

- Acrylic paint.

- Dried green moss.

- Dried or silk flowers.

- Glue and glue gun.

Use the acrylic paints to decorate the birdhouse any way you wish. I usually like to paint the roof a muted a gray, and will color the body of the house a brighter blue. If you plan to install your birdhouse outside, you'll want to use at least a couple coats of paint and carefully cover every exterior surface, to protect it against weathering.

Let each coat dry thoroughly before proceeding with the next. Depending on how involved you want to get, you can add window and doorframe details in a darker shade or a contrasting color. You can also paint a tree against one side of the house, or any other figures or designs that strike your fancy.

Cut the dried green moss into chunks and glue spots of it to the top peak of the roof. You can also use patches of moss at the base of the house to indicate the presence of grass. Glue dried or silk flowers to the roof or on the walls. I have painted little hearts on the sides of my bird houses, but you can paint a tree, a bird, or anything else that suits your fancy. If you want, you can even paint window boxes and attach flowers so that they appear to be growing out of the boxes.

Painted Canvas Shoes

Express yourself; paint your tennies

Yes, you can paint shoes and they will look great for a long time. White shoes are the best, because you do not need to apply as much paint. Thick paint tends to crack and flake, but with white shoes you won't need to apply multiple layers to get the shades you want.

You will need:

- Shoes, preferably white in color.

- Acrylic primer (all-purpose wall primer or gesso).

- Acrylic paints.

- Painter's tape.

- Black permanent marker.

- Pencil.

- Acrylic paintbrushes.

- Disposable plastic plate.

- Water.

- Scotchgard.

Cover whatever you don't want to be painted with painter's tape. That usually means covering the rubber sidewall that goes down to the sole. Cover the soles too, just to be safe. You'll also want to remove the laces before you start painting.

Prime the shoes with wall primer or gesso and let it them dry for at least three hours. Next, paint lightly over the surface with primer, allowing the rough fabric texture to come through the paint.

To prepare a background, place some of your color on the plastic plate and add water to thin it. Brush the background color on evenly. Let it dry for at least six hours.

Trace your design on the shoes very lightly with pencil, then start in with your acrylic colors. You can outline features and add shadow or fine details with your permanent marker.

When you are finished, let the shoes dry for 12 hours. Spray them with Scotchgard per the manufacturer's instructions. After the shoes are thoroughly dry, remove the painter's tape and, voila, you have a work of art you can wear on your feet!

Painted Clay Flower Pots

It is possible to paint terra cotta or clay pots, as long as you seal them afterwards. You can paint stripes using painter's tape to keep them straight, or you can just freehand draw it without worrying about precision. You can also paint figures, animals, or abstract art on the pots, as you wish. You are only limited by your imagination.

Add color to your rooms by painting your flower pots.

You will need:

- Clay pots.

- Plastic disposable plate.

- Brushes and foam sponges on a stick.

- Acrylic paint.

- Clear acrylic spray.

Clean even new pots in soap and warm water. Scrub them with a stiff brush, rinse them off, and let them air dry for at least 24 hours.

Next, you will apply your base coat. Squeeze out some paint onto a plastic plate and add water, mixing with a paintbrush. Apply one coat to the pot and let it dry before and adding a second coat.

After your base coat has dried thoroughly you can add in your details, using any number of colors. When you are finished, let the pots dry for 24 hours before spraying with acrylic sealant. Let this the sealant dry for 24 hours before using the pots.

Painted Glass Jars

I like to spray paint the outside of canning jars. You can use any kind of wide-mouthed jar. Spray painting gives them a frosted look. I use these jars for a variety of purposes such as candle holders, storage jars, and pencil cups.

You will need:

- Spray paint.

- Mason jars.

- Poster board.

- Painter's tape.

- An old cardboard box.

- Small pillar candles (optional, for candle holder

- Stencils.

- Paint, stencils, or sponge brushes.

Clean the jars well by wiping them down with rubbing alcohol and letting them dry at least a couple hours. Cut a shape from the poster board and tape it by folding painter's tape over to make a ring and sticking it tightly against the glass. Set the jar inside a box and spray paint it there to minimize the overspray. I actually recommend using spray paint outdoors, whenever possible. Let the jar dry completely, for 24 to 48 hours. Remove the shape and you'll see a clear spot on the jar that will shine when a candle is lit inside it. Variations on this process could include stenciling on the jar or hand painting it.

Painted Glass Plates

It is possible to paint on clear glass, but you generally must be very careful when you wash it. You cannot put this in a dishwasher and must carefully rinse painted glass items in warm – not hot – water, or the paint may come off.

You will need:

- Clear glass plate.

- Glass paint.

- Glass stencil.

- Glass squeegee.

- Paper towels.

You can find specialized glass stencils at your craft store. They have an adhesive backing that makes it easy to apply to the plate. Of course, you can always paint the plate freehand, or embellish your stencil work with freehand flourishes.

Clean the plate with soap and water and let it dry completely. Take a cotton pad and rub the plate, front and back, with rubbing alcohol. Let it dry. Peel the backing from the glass stencil and apply to the plate per instructions on the stencil. Rub out any air bubbles. Apply a line of glass paint above the design but on the stencil; it doesn't take much. Use the little squeegee to draw the paint down over the stencil. Let the paint dry a little and remove the stencil while it is still a bit wet. Clean the stencil in water. Let the paint dry completely and embellish it as you wish, with a brush and more paint. If you use multiple colors, allow one color to dry completely before adding another.

Cure the plate by placing it in a cool oven, heating the oven on to 350 degrees Fahrenheit, and letting it set there for 30 minutes. Turn off the oven and let the plate completely cool to room temperature before removing it.

Carefully remove the plate after cooling and allow it to set undisturbed for a full seven hours. This curing process will allow you to safely hand wash the plate without removing the paint. There is no guarantee your paint will stay on if you air dry it without curing the paint. Never use glitter paint if you are putting the plate in the oven.

Painted Pail/Watering Can

These can provide a touch of whimsy on your front porch or patio, while still serving functionally to hold water. You can use them as pots for plants or to hold flowers as you cut them.

You will need:

- Aluminum or metal watering can or bucket.

- White vinegar.

- Metal spray paint and primer (don't use oil-based primer because it reacts with the metal).

84

- Sandpaper.

- Paintbrushes.

- Acrylic paint for embellishments.

You can use new or used cans or pails but they must be clean and dry. Apply white vinegar to the surface you plan to paint and let it air dry. This application of an acid reacts with the metal and helps the paint stick.

If you are using an old can, use sandpaper to remove rust and smooth out any rough patches. Prime the object, allow it to dry, and then spray paint the entire surface. After the base coat is completely dry, you can use acrylic paint to add flowers, hearts, or other motifs. Let the paint dry completely before using.

Painted Plastic Tub

You can paint plastic tubs, buckets, or watering cans about as easily as their metal counterparts. Painted tubs will add a touch of fun wherever they are used. You can paint them a solid color or add motifs with acrylic paint and a paintbrush. You can also make the tub striped by marking it with painter's tape.

You will need:

- Fine sandpaper or steel wool.

- Spray on primer.

- Spray paint.

- Acrylic paint.

- Painter's tape.

- Brush.

Clean the tub with soap and water. Rub it with sandpaper or steel wool until smooth, then wipe it down well. Paint with plastic primer and let it dry. A primer is important to prevent the paint from flaking off and fading prematurely.

Cover the primer coat with spray paint and let it dry for about 24 hours. Then, you can decorate your tub with acrylic paint. Painters' tape is highly useful if you want to make stripes or other patterns. You can also create a chalkboard surface on the tub by applying three or four coats of chalkboard paint.

Painted Stair Risers

Painted stair risers, on a grand scale

This is more of a home improvement project than a craft, but it does look crafty. If you have wooden stairs, you can paint the risers and make them look special. The risers are the vertical part of the stairs that connect the flat steps.

You can choose from one of these projects or invent your own:

86

1. Paint each riser a different color. Use indoor latex paint that you can get in sample cans.

2. Paint the risers a solid color and stencil numbers on them.

3. Paint clouds and stars on the risers to depict a "stairway to heaven."

4. Paint book bindings as if the risers are bookshelves and label them with your favorite book titles and authors, or fanciful titles and authors, if you wish.

5. Paint animals like cats, ducks, birds, fish, and other whimsical characters on the risers.

6. Paint a checkerboard on each riser using painter's tape to keep everything straight.

7. Paint hearts on the risers.

8. Use a professional stencil or make your own to use on the risers.

Before starting to paint your risers, you must make sure the wood is clean. Wipe them down with a wood washing liquid and let them dry thoroughly. If the risers are varnished or painted, you may need to use a little sandpaper to roughen the surface; and then clean off the dust well before you proceed.

Starting at the top of the stairs, you'll work your way down. If the wood is bare, you'll want to use a primer to ensure that the paint sticks evenly to the risers. Use painter's tape and drop cloths to protect the stair steps and neighboring walls from errant paint. Use a roller or a two-inch brush to apply the paint.

Painted Tote Bag

Pick up a fabric tote bag at the craft store and paint it to suit your personality.

You will need the following basics:

- A fabric tote bag – I prefer muslin bags, but canvas or cotton work well, too.

- Iron and ironing board.

- Fabric paint.

- Paintbrush or sponge.

Wash the tote bag first to get rid of the finish that makes the bag feel crisp; it also prevents paint from adhering properly to the fabric. Iron your dry tote bag until there are no wrinkles.

At this point you can use fabric paints to draw freehand or stencil images on the bag.

Painted Two-Liter Bottle Butterflies

This is a fun craft that uses some recycled items.
You will need:
- An empty clear two-liter bottle with the labels removed

- Acrylic paint.

- Marker.

- Scissors or craft knife.

- Fishing line.

- 2 large beads, five medium- sized beads, and a bunch of seed beads.

- Quick-drying strong glue.

Cut the top and bottom off a two-liter bottle, then cut down the side where the label was glued on. Uncurl the plastic and lay it flat on your work surface. Take a marker, and draw on the bottle a pair of butterfly wings that are connected in the middle, and cut them out. They will bend, which is what we want. Paint the wings any way you wish.

Take a long piece of fishing line, thread on one seed bead and fold the line in half, moving that the bead to the center of the fishing line. Tie a knot so that one side half of the line goes through the bead and the other half runs outside above it. Tie a knot just below the bead; this will keep the rest of the beads aligned. Take the two sides of the line and thread four more medium-sized beads through the doubled-over fishing line, followed by the two large beads.

Separate the two strands of fishing line, threading a seed bead on each. Place a small dot of glue over the top of the seed beads where the fishing line comes out. Cut the line so that about one inch protrudes beyond the seed beads. This is will serve as the butterfly's antennae.

Once the wings have dried completely, fold them upward, then attach them with heavy-duty glue to the bead-body along the fold the butterfly. The wings should curve inward. The five medium beads are the body and the two large beads make up the head.

Painted Tin Cans

Tin cans paint up rather nicely with the help of spray paint. You can embellish the base coat with acrylic paint if you want. These cans can be used to hold utensils, pens, pencils, or as candle holders.

One of my favorite crafts with painted cans is to make ghosts or jack-o-lanterns at Halloween. I spray paint the cans orange for the Jack-o-lanterns and white for the ghosts. I use black acrylic paint and a paintbrush to add eyes, nose, and mouth after the spray paint dries.

You can decorate your can any way you want; flowers, hearts, polka dots, or other motifs work equally well. You can use these cans to store tacks, nails, candy, rubber bands, paperclips, or pretty much anything your heart desires.

Painted Rocks

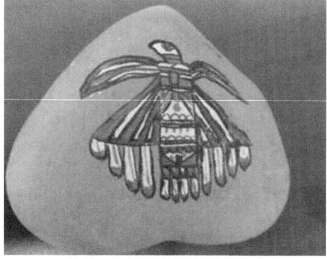

Native Design Painted On Rock

I love to paint rocks. Because each rock is unique, the decorating possibilities are endless. You can paint animals on them, mandalas, flowers, or abstract shapes. I use small rocks and paint fairy faces on them, scattering them about so that kids in the neighborhood can discover them.

For this project you will need smooth round rocks; the best are beach rocks or river stones. You can find these rocks at the beach, along a stream, in a craft store, or even online.

You will need:

- Small smooth rocks.

- Acrylic paint.

- Paintbrushes and sponges.

- Mod Podge or clear acrylic spray.

Prepare your rocks by washing them well and letting them dry overnight. You can sketch out what you want to do using a piece of chalk, but I usually draw my work freehand.

Paint your rock however you wish. Let it dry for 24 hours, then seal the paint with a layer of Mod Podge or a clear acrylic spray. Don't paint the bottom of the rock; it will dry faster with one side left open to the air.

Pallet Sign Post

These sign posts look cute on a family room wall or down in a rec room. You can easily customize your creations. The pallet boards serve as travel signs.

You will need:

- Pallet, deconstructed.

- Saw.

- Nails and hammer or staples and staple gun.

- Old paintbrushes or paint sponges.

- Acrylic paint.

Take a pallet apart and keep several of the top boards. Use one of the thinner boards for the signpost or use a two by four that is long enough to accommodate all the signs.

Take a saw and cut one end of several pallet boards into "v" shapes, so they look like pointing arrows. You can paint the boards different colors or leave them plain. If you use a two by four for the vertical post, paint it to look old and scuffed up like the rest of the pallet boards.

After the painted boards are dry, come back and paint names of towns and how many miles it takes to get there. If your family is from Ohio, you can make a sign that shows the name of the town they hail from, along with a fictitious amount of miles to get there. If you have always wanted to go to Hollywood, California, make a sign for it. Once the signs are dry, attach them to the vertical board with nails or a staple gun. The signs don't have to be straight; a little random crookedness only adds to the charm.

Add a picture hanger to the back and hang your creation on the wall.

Pallet Wall Hanging

Pallet art is very a rustic form of household décor. It is so popular that I have included several additional pallet projects in the wood crafts chapter of this book.

In this project you will use a pallet to create an interesting focal point on one of your interior walls.

You will need:

- Pieces of a pallet.

- Saw.

- 4 two by fours.

- Nail and hammer.

- Old paintbrushes or sponge brushes.

- Acrylic paint.

There's no need to make everything perfectly straight, even, or smooth. Because the wood is rough, you'll want to use old brushes or sponges. Pull off three boards from the front of the pallet and cut them with a saw to about the same length, if they aren't already the same. It is ok if they have jagged edges.

Use two by fours or smaller boards from the pallet to nail the pieces together. Lay down the thin boards vertically, so they are about five to six inches away from the edges of the pallet pieces. They will form the structural support that holds the horizontal boards together. Nail each of the boards in place close together. Trim off the thin boards so they don't protrude beyond the horizontal boards.

Painting on pallet wood is not easy to do; it is rough, unprimed, and unsanded, so you'll need to scrub to push the paint into the wood. Even so, much of the wood grain will show through the paint because the wood is so weathered. That's as it should be.

The top board will represent the sky, with light blue and fluffy white clouds. The middle board will be mostly water, so paint it with a greenish blue and let a little go down to the top of the bottom board. The rest of the bottom board will be a sand color. Once this paint is dry, you can paint in the details of waves, stones, seagulls and the like. Let the piece dry. Attach a hanging wire to the vertical pieces in the back and hang this on the wall.

Repurposed, Painted Baby Wipes Containers

Plastic baby wipes containers make wonderful holders for fabric softener sheets, pencils, cotton balls, pins, you name it. Remove the labels from your container, and paint the plastic all over the outside, using a spray primer. Model paint works well to hand paint with figures, letters, or numbers. Let your creativity soar as you paint anything that suits your fancy.

Small Pallet Wall Hanging

Pallets usually measure 48 by 40 inches, but you can find half-pallets and others that are much smaller. The 36-inch square pallets are perfect for this project.

You will need:

- 3 large or 9 small pallets

- Acrylic or latex interior/exterior paint

- Old paint paintbrushes or paint sponges

- Screws, drill, and wire to hang pallets

This makes a great piece of wall art; depending on the amount of space you wish to cover, you can complete this project by using three, six, or nine pallets.

Paint each pallet a different color. I like to use exterior house paint because it covers a little bit easier. Apply one to three coats, depending on how rough you want your signs to appear. Many paint stores sell sample cans of paint; that's what usually use. I've also used clearance stocks of discarded paint, sold cheap at hardware stores. Sometimes I've been able to relieve friends and neighbors of old paint they have no use for.

Use a drill to install screws on the back of the pallets on either side. Do not screw them all the way through. Take heavy wire and wrap it around the screw heads, then screw them tightly into the pallet to hold the wire securely. You will have one on each side with the wire going from one screw to the other. Hang the pallet on the wall from this wire.

Place the pallets three across or add a row underneath. You can even use three rows of three pallets if you want.

Spattered Stained Glass Vase

This project is similar to the stained vase project earlier, but the technique is slightly different.

You will need:

- A clear glass vase.

- Glass stain.

- Paper towels.

- A paintbrush.

- An empty cardboard box to contain the spatter.

Clean the outside of the vase with soap and water, rinse well, and let it dry. Use a cotton pad to wipe the outside surface with alcohol, then let it air dry completely.

Set the vase upside down in the box that has been turned on its side. This will prevent the paint from getting everywhere. If you can do your painting outside, all the better.

Dip your brush in the paint and flick it toward the vase. The paint will stick to the outside of the vase, allowing the spatter to target the sides. It is best to turn the vase upside down so that none of the paint goes inside. You can do each color separately and let the paint dry between color applications. You can also apply all the colors at one time. In this case, you'll want to use the lighter colors first.

Spray-Painted Circle Art

When you use metallic spray paint, this makes quite a statement in your living room.

You will need:

- Raised canvas.

- Poster board.

- Spray paint.

- Glue.

- Scissors.

Cut uniform circles from poster board. You will need enough to completely cover the canvas, with some overlap. The circles at the top, bottom, and either side edge of the canvas must be cut in half so they fit against the edges while the rest will be full circles. Spray-paint the circles one or more colors. Start gluing them down in the middle of the canvas, using full circles. Place one dead center and then overlap and glue the next as you work out toward the sides. When you reach an edge, glue a half circle with the flat side against the edge of the canvas. Keep on gluing circles until you reach both the top and bottom of the canvas. Use half circles at the top and bottom.

Striped Painted Initials Letters

Hang these letters on a wall, over an interior door, or glue them to a bed headboard.

You will need:

- Wooden letters.

- Acrylic craft paint.

- Foam brush.

- Painter's tape.

Use painter's tape to make uniform stripes the width of the tape. Measure down to where the second color will appear on the letter and apply the painter's tape. Paint the top of the letter above the tape one color.

Wait one hour for the paint to dry and look to see if it needs a second coat. After this paint is completely dry, place a piece of tape over what you just painted and another strip a ways below the first strip of tape you applied. Remove the first strip of tape and paint a second color, add a second coat as needed, and let this dry. Continue all down and around each letter, creating a rainbow of stripes on the letters.

Swirled Stained Glass Vase

Glass stain can be obtained at most craft stores and the swirling action of the stain makes can make for a very pretty translucent colored vase that is clear yet colored.

You will need:

- A clear glass vase.

- Glass stain.

- Paper towels.

Clean the inside of the glass vase with soap and water, rinse well, and let it dry. Use a cotton pad to wipe the interior surface with alcohol, and then let it air dry completely.

Take a generous amount of glass stain and place a line of stain on the inside lip of the vase. Swirl the vase around, allowing the stain to flow downward and around until it nears the bottom of the vase. If necessary, introduce additional stain until there's enough to cover most of the vase.

Do not mix wet colors. If you want a multi- colored vase, allow one color to dry completely before you apply another.

When you are satisfied with the stain's coverage of the vase, turn it upside down over a paper towel to let any excess stain pour out. Turn the vase upright again and allow it to dry for seven hours.

Watercolor Phrase Wall Hanging

Phrase art looks lovely on the walls along with paintings. You can put your favorite quote up on the wall, and surround it with family pictures if you want.

You will need:

- Watercolors in tubes.

- Watercolor paper.

- Pencil.

- Painter's tape.

- Masking fluid.

- Artist's brush.

- A wooden board.

- A chosen phrase or quote.

- Water.

- Plastic disposable plate.

- Sponge.

Choose a phrase and print it by hand or on your printer. I've used "Beauty is in the eye of the beholder." Tape your phrase to a window on a sunny day and tape the watercolor paper on top of it. Trace the phrase lightly with a pencil, then remove everything from the window.

On your watercolor paper, fill in the text with masking fluid. You can find this in the art section of a craft store. Let it dry until it is tacky. Now tape the paper to a piece of wood. Put a desired color of watercolor on the plate and add enough water to make it liquid. Splash the paint over and around the phrase. Use a sponge to wet a small area and mix it to spread the paint. You will notice that the masking fluid has developed a skin and the paint will not seep under it. The fluid is protecting the phrase from the paint so use as much paint as you want and mix it to your delight. Let the project dry thoroughly. Rub the masking fluid near the beginning or end of the phrase and carefully pull it off. Your project is ready to frame.

Chapter 5: Fragrant Crafts

CANDLEMAKING

Candles are fun and easy to make, but you must be ever mindful of the heat factor. Wax is melted in order to make candles and that can be dangerous, especially around children.

Soap is often made with caustic materials, but the soap crafts in this book are not made with lye. They are safe; some will, however, require heat to melt them in the process of shaping the soaps. The other fragrant crafts include potpourri and air fresheners.

You will need several essential oils for these projects. Avoid synthetic oils or fragrance oils; these do not hold the scent as effectively as essential oils. They are also more likely to spark allergic reactions than are the essential oils. Essential oils come from the plant itself. If you want your soap to smell like lavender, the lavender essential oil is a product of the lavender plant itself, not a synthetic chemical.

Any pans, bowls, or other utensils you use for making candles, soap, or potpourri should never be used to cook; the oils and wax will remain in them and these flavors will be passed on to your food. You can fairly cheaply find used utensils for this craft work by visiting a thrift store or a few garage sales.

A Word About Wax

Paraffin is the most common wax used in candle making. It melts quickly and is inexpensive. It colors and scents easily, but when it melts it does release a chemical into the air that bothers some individuals. Paraffin catches fire easily. It melts at about 140 degrees, Fahrenheit.

About 20 ounces of liquid wax is needed to make a decent sized candle. It will take about 24 hours for this amount of paraffin to dry.

Soy wax is made from soybeans and is considered highly eco-friendly. It burns slowly but is a little more expensive than paraffin, so the cost equals out in the end. Soy melts at about 170 degrees Fahrenheit and requires four to five hours to dry. It takes about 18 ounces of liquid wax to make a candle.

Beeswax is a natural wax that burns quickly and looks pretty. Of the three options, it is the healthiest. Beeswax actually purifies the air as it burns. However, it is very difficult to work with.

Beeswax melts at 145 to 170 degrees Fahrenheit. It tends to burn hot and fast. A workaround is to mix a half cup of coconut oil into a pound of beeswax. This effectively lowers the burning temperature, making your candles burn longer. Keep in mind, though that this mixture does not keep its shape well; it is best poured into a glass jar and burned right there.

You will need about 16 ounces of beeswax to make a candle and it will take more than six hours to dry. Another challenge is that beeswax does not color or scent easily.

The Basics Of Molded Candles

Basic candle items:

- Double boiler.

- Thermometer.

- Scissors.

- Needle nose pliers.

- Wax.

- Wicks, preferably 30-ply cotton braided wick #4.

- Molds.

- Craft sticks or chopsticks.

- Pencil.

Wicks come in two parts. There is usually a metal flat piece that sets on the bottom and holds the wick upright. You assemble a wick by pushing it into the metal tab and pinching it shut with pliers. You will want your wick to extend at least an inch above the top of the candle mold.

Melt your wax in a double boiler with water in the bottom container. You should cool the wax slightly before you pour it into a mold. If you are adding essential oils or color (only use color tabs found in craft stores for making candles), let the wax cool to 125 degrees Fahrenheit before you add them. Then mix these additives into the wax by stirring with a wooden craft stick. Never add color or scent while the wax is boiling because it will evaporate with the steam.

Carefully push the wick's metal tab and the attached wick down in the center of the mold. Use a wooden chopstick or craft stick to push it down to the bottom. Lay a pencil or clean chopstick across the top center of the mold and wrap the top of the wick over this to keep it centered. Pour the melted wax into the mold and let the candle cool completely before removing it.

There are other things you can use as molds in addition to the items you can buy in a craft store. Most common are tin cans and paper milk cartons. Just peel the milk carton off once the candle has cooled completely.

You can melt down old candles to make new ones. Old candles will melt down at about 185 degrees F, but the colors will mix. Who knows what color you'll end up with?

Canning Jar Luminaries

These luminaries can transform your driveway or front sidewalk into a wonderland. They will enhance an evening wedding, lending a warm glow to church or outdoor venue alike. Spread across a lawn, they lend an ethereal quality to an evening party. And there is nothing more welcoming to your guests than to be led to your door along a path of gleaming light.

You will need:

- Quart jars.

- White sand.

- Votive candles.

Pour two inches of sand in the bottom of the jar and place a votive candle in the center. Place and light it; it's that simple.

To add variety, you can use colored sand or create your own votive candles using the basic candle information provided earlier in this chapter. You can use pint jars to house your luminaries and tealights instead of votives. You can paint designs on the jars before using them. The best thing about these luminaries is that you can keep and reuse them forever.

Glass Jar Candles

You will need:

- Basic candle items.

- Pint-sized glass jars.

Use the basic candle recipe to make candles and pour them into mason jars that have a wick suspended from the center. The clear glass allows the candle light to radiate freely as the candle burns down in the jar.

Layered Glass Candle

Add interest to your candles by layering colors.

You will need:

- Basic candle items.

- Large glass container.

You'll prepare smaller quantities of melted wax, each one a different color. For example, you could make a red, white, and blue candle for patriotic holidays. Pour the red wax into the glass container first. Let this cool completely. Your next layer will have no color at all. Just pour the melted wax in and let it cool completely. Next prepare the blue and pour it on top of the uncolored, white wax. Let it cool completely.

As always, the sky's the limit with the color combinations you can use. You can use as many or as few layers as you wish. You can vary their thicknesses. You can give each color a different fragrance, so that the candle will smell differently as it reaches a different layer. You can tilt the jar one direction for one layer and the opposite direction for the next layer, creating diagonal lines in addition to straight horizontal layers. Feel free to experiment to your heart's content.

Painted Pillars

You can paint existing candles with acrylic craft paint or candle paint, transforming plain wax into gleaming delights. I painted hearts on pillar candles for Valentine's Day and have transformed plain cylinders into evergreen trees for Christmas.

You will need:

- Pillar candle.

- Rubbing alcohol.

- Lint-free cloth.

- Artist brushes.

- Acrylic craft paint.

- Candle painting medium.

- Disposable plastic plate.

Mix equal parts of the acrylic paint with candle painting medium and mix with a brush on a plastic plate. Paint your design on the candle letting each color dry before applying the next. Limit your decorations to the sides of the candle; never paint near the wick.

Paper Napkin Candle

You will use a pillar candle purchased at your local discount store for this craft. Use either a pretty paper napkin or tissue paper to make this beautiful candle.

You will need:

- White pillar candle.

- Napkin or tissue paper.

- Iron.

If you're using a two-ply napkin, peel apart the layers and use only the pretty ply of the napkin. Wrap it around the pillar candle. Set your iron to warm and carefully press the napkin onto the candle, rotating it until you've covered all sides of the candle. The heat from the iron will melt the candle, slightly soaking the paper napkin with wax and making it part of the candle.

As an alternative method, you can cut the napkin into pieces or strips and iron down each piece. When you are finished, trim the napkin edges even with the candle. You'll also want to clean any remaining wax off the iron while it is warm.

Paper Napkin Candle, Alternative Method

This method doesn't require an iron, but can be just as attractive. Instead of melting the napkin to the candle, you use Mod Podge to affix the paper. The Mod Podge lends a light sheen to your candle surface when it is dry.

You will need:

- White pillar candle.

- Napkins or tissue paper.

- Foam brush.

- Mod Podge.

- Scissors.

Only use one ply of your napkin. Place the napkin flat against the candle's side. Paint over it with generous amounts of Mod Podge, effectively gluing the napkin to the candle. You'll want to push any air bubbles out, leaving the napkin flush against the candle surface. It's easiest to work a section at a time making sure there are no bubbles. Trim the napkin flush against the top edge of the candle and let it dry completely before using.

Pressed Flower And Herbs Glass Candle

You can use any kind of wide-mouthed glass container for this project.

You will need:

- Basic candle items.

- Glass jar.

- Pressed herbs and flowers.

- Tweezers.

- Flat artist's brush.

Turn your jar on the side and place pressed herbs and flowers against the glass inside on the bottom. Hold them down with tweezers. Dip your paintbrush in melted wax and paint the herbs and flowers onto the side of the jar with the wax. Do this all the way around the jar.

Let the wax dry so that when you stand the jar upright, the herbs and flowers will stay put. Carefully pour the rest of the wax in the jar and proceed to place the wick. Usually the herbs and flowers will shift slightly when the wax is poured in, but they will remain pretty close to where you placed them.

Teacup Candle

You will need:

- Basic candle items.

- Old teacup and saucer.

- Superglue.

You can find old teacups and saucers at flea markets, thrift stores, or garage sales. Superglue the saucer to the cup and pour the wax into the teacup, adding a wick to the center.

SOAP

Making your own soap is fun and you can always customize it to your needs and preferences. The following are several different nontoxic soap recipes. Always use pans and utensils that are dedicated to this purpose and do not mix them with candle making equipment or potpourri utensils. Most certainly do not use them for cooking.

You can purchase soap molds at a craft store. Silicone molds are very easy to use and I prefer them over any other. The molds come in floral, animal, or geometric shapes or you can find forms for rectangular or oval bars. I actually use silicone cupcake pans, mostly because they are cheap and the resulting soap will fit perfectly into your hand. You will fill cupcake molds three quarters of the way and let the soaps cure before popping them out.

Herb Lemon Soap

Glycerin soap comes in small blocks that melt readily in the microwave.

You will need:

- 2 pounds glycerin soap.

- Several sprigs of fresh herbs like basil, mint, or rosemary.

- Essential oils of lemon and orange.

Melt your glycerin soap in a microwave in 30-second intervals, stirring between shots of heat. While you are melting the glycerin, puree the herb sprigs and squeeze out any excess liquid by wrapping the puree in a paper towel. You will need to add one tablespoon of herb mixture for each cup of melted glycerin. Let the glycerin cool five minutes before adding the herbs. Add 10 drops of lemon essential oil and five drops of orange, stirring well. Pour this liquid into molds and let it set in the freezer for one hour.

Lavender Rosemary Bars

Essential oils add fragrance to your soaps.

You will need:

- 1/4 cup extra virgin coconut oil.

- 1/4 cup shea butter.

- 1/4 cup beeswax.

- 1 Craft stick.

- 1/4 teaspoon vitamin E oil.

- Lavender and rosemary essential oils.

- Soap dye (optional).

Place water in the bottom of a double boiler, then put the oil, shea butter and grated wax in the top section. Warm over medium high heat. When the water begins to boil, remove the double boiler from the fire and stir the contents until the mixture is completely melted.

Add the vitamin E oil, 14 drops of lavender oil, and 10 drops of rosemary oil. Mix well by stirring with a craft stick. If you choose to color your soap, purchase soap dye and add a little, again stirring with the craft stick to blend well. Then pour the liquid into the molds. This soap looks nice in a light purple or green, matching the fragrance choice.

Lemon Soap

If you find lemonade refreshing, you'll be equally revitalized by this soap!

You will need:

- 15 cubes of shea butter soap base.

- 4 to 6 drops of lemon essential oil.

- Dried zest of three lemons.

If the soap base comes in cubes, chop them up a bit and put into a glass measuring cup. Microwave at 30-second intervals until completely melted. Add the lemon essential oil along with the zest and stir well. Pour this liquid into molds and allow your soap to harden for at least one hour.

Oatmeal Soap

Oatmeal is reported to have a skin-softening effect; it also will soothe irritated skin.

You will need:

- 8 cubes shea butter base.

- Sweet almond oil soap extract.

- 1/4 cup old-fashioned oats, chopped fine in a blender.

Chop the soap base cubes and place into a large glass measuring cup. Microwave in 30-second intervals until completely melted. Add 40 drops of almond oil extract. Add a quarter cup of oats, mix well, and pour into molds. Let these cool and solidify before removing from the molds.

Pumpkin Pie Soap

No, this soap isn't made with pumpkin, but it smells like pumpkin pie. The trick is the pumpkin pie spice you can find in any grocery store. Purchase soap bases in a craft store.

You will need:

- 2 pounds shea butter soap base.

- Red and yellow soap dye.

- 2 tablespoons pumpkin pie spice.

Place the soap base in a four-cup glass measuring cup. Microwave in 30-second intervals, stirring with a craft stick until completely melted. Stir in two drops of yellow soap dye and one drop of red dye; this will yield a warm orange-beige color. Add the pumpkin pie spice and mix in well. Pour into molds and let it cool to room temperature before removing.

SCRUBS

Scrubs are a type of soap that removes dirt and oils as it exfoliates the skin. They are designed for use on hands and feet primarily, although they can be used very gently on your whole body and extremely lightly on your face.

Scrubs get their abrasiveness from sugar or salt. They are stored at room temperature and will last about one month before they start to go moldy. Store this soap in small jars with a lid.

To use it, scoop out a small amount of the scrub onto the palm of your hand. Add a little water and mix it in. Apply this to your body, scrub lightly, and rinse off with cool water.

Coffee Scrub

You will need:

- 1 cup coconut oil.

- 1/2 cup sugar.

- 1/3 cup fresh coffee grounds.

- 3 tablespoons olive oil.

Mix everything together and store it in a jar.

Lavender Scrub

You will need:

- 2 cups sugar.

- 1 cup grapeseed oil.

- 1 teaspoon vanilla extract.

- 2 tablespoons dried lavender flowers.

- 10 drops lavender essential oil.

Mix everything together and store it in a jar.

Lemon Scrub

You will need:

- 1/2 cup sea salt.

- 1/2 cup olive oil.

- 2 slices of lemon.

- 2 slices of orange.

Place the salt and olive oil in a blender. With a knife, chop the fruit and add to the blender. After blending thoroughly, pour the resulting mixture into a jar.

Mint Sugar Scrub

You will need:

- 1 cup sugar.

- 1 tablespoon dry milk.

- 1/2 cup coconut oil.

- 1/4 teaspoon mint extract (used in cooking).

Mix all the ingredients together with a craft stick.

Sugar Olive Oil Scrub

You will need:

- 3 tablespoons extra virgin olive oil.

- 2 tablespoons honey.

- 1/2 cup sugar.

Combine the olive oil and honey in a jar and add sugar, stirring with a wooden craft stick. When everything is well mixed, put a lid on the jar and you're ready to go.

FRAGRANCES

It's time to scent your atmosphere. You can easily create diffusers and potpourri that will keep your house smelling fresh. These are excellent crafts to make as gifts.

Baking Soda Scent

Baking soda removes nasty odors from the air; this diffuser will keep your kitchen and bathroom smelling sweet without overly perfuming the air.

You will need:

- 1/2 cup baking soda.

- 8 to 10 drops of a favorite essential oil.

- Scrapbook paper.

- Canning jar with ring.

- Pencil.

- Scissors.

- Tapestry needle.

Place the scrapbook paper face down on a flat surface and trace around the inside of the screw lid. Cut out the paper a little bit larger than your tracing and poke a few holes in the paper with the tapestry needle.

Mix the baking soda in the jar along with the essential oils. Set the paper over the mouth of the jar and screw on the ring. To use this powder, shake out some of the baking soda onto carpets, let it set for a few minutes, then vacuum it up.

Gel Diffuser

You will need:

- Saucepan.

- 35 drops essential oil.

- Pint canning jar.

- 1 cup water.

- 4 packets of unflavored gelatin.

- Wire whisk.

- 1 cup cold water.

- 1 tablespoon salt.

- Nylon net cut two times the size of the jar mouth.

- Screw ring for jar.

Put 35 drops of essential oil into the jar and set it aside. Boil one cup of water in a saucepan, remove it from the heat and pour in the packages of gelatin. Whisk continually to prevent clumping. When the gelatin has dissolved completely, add the cold water and the salt. Stir everything well, then pour it into the jar. Let this rest overnight, until the substance has set (it will be solid but with some jiggle to it) Place the nylon net circle over the jar and screw it on with the ring.

Rice Diffuser

Never use minute rice in this craft because it will not hold the scent.

You will need:

- 1/2 cup jasmine rice, uncooked.

- 20 drops of your favorite essential oil.

- Craft stick to mix.

- Pint canning jar with ring.

- Nylon netting.

- Scissors.

- Ribbon.

Place the rice in a bowl and add the essential oil. Mix with the craft stick and pour into a pint canning jar. Cut a round piece of nylon netting twice the size of the mouth of your jar. Lay the netting over the jar's mouth and screw down the ring. This will keep kids and animals out of the diffuser. You can tie a silk ribbon around the ring to cover it, if you wish.

Wood Block Diffuser

Wood blocks can hold the scent of essential oils, releasing the fragrance over time. Any wood you use should be plain and natural with no treatments, stain, or paint added.

You will need:

- Several wood blocks.

- Artist's brush.

- Essential oil of your choice.

- Reclosable plastic bag.

Paint the essential oil on all sides of a block and then let it set, closed up in the plastic bag, for 10 hours. After this time you can remove the block and set it on a shelf, allowing space on all sides for air circulation. It will scent the room for about two weeks. After that time, you can rejuvenate the fragrance by adding more drops of essential oil to the wood.

POTPOURRI

Crock-Pot Potpourri

This works the same way as the simmering potpourri but you don't have to worry about a pot drying out on the stove. Purchase a small Crock-Pot and use it just for potpourri.

You will need:

- 1/2 orange, sliced.

- Whole cinnamon sticks, broken.

- 1/2 cup whole cranberries.

- 1 teaspoon whole cloves.

- 1 teaspoon nutmeg.

Fill the small Crock-Pot up to two inches below the rim with water and add the rest of the ingredients. Simmer on high for about one hour and then reduce the temperature to the low setting. Add water as needed. You'll want to use your Crock-Pot for no more than eight hours at a stretch; never leave it on overnight.

Dry Potpourri

Dry potpourri in a sachet bag can add clean fragrance to a closet or drawer.

Everything in a dry potpourri must be completely dry to prevent mold from appearing. Beyond that, you can use almost anything organic in the mix. Flower petals will often retain the fragrance of the fresh blooms, but even wood shavings can be infused with essential oils to release fragrant aroma into a room.

Rose Spice Potpourri

You will need:

- 2 cups dried rose petals.

- 2 cups dried carnation petals.

- 1/2 cup orris root.

- 1 whole cinnamon stick.

- 2 whole cloves.

- 5 drops rose essential oil.

Mix all the ingredients well in a glass dish or a canning jar. Secure the netting over the top of the bowl with a rubber band. If you place your potpourri in a glass canning jar, simply screw the ring down over the netting. This will keep pets and children out of the potpourri mixture.

Dry potpourri lasts about one to two months and can be easily refreshed by adding a little more essential oil. Part of the refreshing quality of potpourri is its appearance. In addition to the colorful petals, you can cut up or curl colorful ribbon or paper to add to the visual appeal.

Simmering Potpourri

Here's an easy way to make your house smell lovely; all you need to do is put a pan on the stove. You can mix the contents this potpourri and store them in a pint jar until you need it. It makes a great gift, offered in a decorative jar along with directions for its use.

You will need:

- Saucepan.

- Water.

- Lemon.

- Rosemary sprigs.

- 1/2 teaspoon vanilla.

Fill a saucepan two-thirds full of water and set it on the stove. Cut your lemon into slices, rind and all, and throw them into the pot. Add the rosemary sprigs and the vanilla. Let the pot simmer and add water before it starts to dry out.

Chapter 6: Wood Crafts

You don't have to be a carpenter to create beautiful things with wood. Craft stores have tons of wood crafts already made, just waiting for you to add the finishing touches. Wood crafts include shelves for your walls, miniature houses, geometric shapes, almost anything you can imagine. All you need to do is paint them and set them in a windowsill or other place where they can be seen and admired.

One of the most important supplies you will need is sandpaper. Wood items always need to be sanded down before you do anything else with them. You will want some medium and fine sandpaper, at the very least. In addition, a sanding block can save your hands and wrists from excess wear and tear.

Another item you will need often is wood glue. Wood glue will be applied and in most cases will need to be clamped down while it dries. In some cases, you can also use hot glue effectively on wood projects.

Balsa Book Cover

A balsa cover can really add some pizzazz to your scrapbooking. You can also use this project to make a handmade journal. You can keep it for yourself or give it to a friend. You'll be making both front and back covers, then binding them to your chosen pages.

You will need:

- balsa sheets (optionally, use a third sheet for ornamentation).

- Craft knife.

- Emery board.

- Ruler.

- Pencil.

- Hammer and nail.

- Nylon or leather string.

- Scissors.

- Paper pages to put between the covers.

Cut two pieces of balsa wood, measuring about one inch larger than the paper you plan to use. Use the emery board to smooth the edges. You can add class to your front cover by gluing strips of contrasting grain or pieces of different colored balsa to the top. You'll want to complete any painting or wood burning embellishments to this cover before you go any further.

Measure down the left side of the cover about three quarters of an inch from the edge. Evenly space where you will place three holes, marking the spot with a pencil. Mark the same hole locations on the back cover. Use a hammer and nail to create holes at the appropriate locations. Punch holes in the paper to match the holes in the covers.

Starting at the bottom hole of the back cover, bring the string up through the bottom hole leaving a 10-inch tail hanging. Thread this string through the bottom hole in the paper and up through the bottom hole of the front cover. Pass the string through the front cover's middle hole, passing it through the paper and the back cover. Then, pass the string back up through the top hole, from back to front. Take the string and bring it down through the middle hole again all the way to the back cover. Turn the book over and securely knot the tail with the end of the string you just passed through to the back. Trim the string so that both tails are even.

Balsa Wood Bookmark

Balsa wood is light, strong, and usually very thin; it is most often used on models and is fairly easy to find in most craft stores. Thin strips of balsa wood can make wonderful bookmarks.

You will need:

- Balsa strip.

- Craft knife.

- Emery board.

- Nail and hammer.

- Ribbon.

- Acrylic paint.

- Clear acrylic spray.

Using a craft knife, cut the balsa wood into a strip about five inches long. It doesn't work to use scissors on balsa wood because it causes the wood to split along the grain. To cut it, score the wood with a sharp knife and bend it until it breaks. You can use the emery board to sand the edges until they are smooth.

Take a nail and hammer it through the top center of the balsa wood, into a block of wood. When you remove the nail, you'll have a neat hole in your bookmark.

Paint the bookmark any way you wish. Balsa is very porous; it will quickly soak up any paint you give it and can warp if it gets too much – so use as little paint as possible. Balsa wood can be easily decorated with a wood burner, though. Just remember it burns faster than more dense woods.

When you're finished decorating your bookmark, cut 10 inches of ribbon, string it through the hole made by the nail and tie the ribbon together. You can braid several ribbons together or make ornamental knots along its length, as you wish.

Chalkboard Town

A chalkboard house can also double as message board.

Use flat houses for this project.

You will need:

- Flat wooden buildings, about one to one and a half inch thick.

- Sandpaper.

- Chalk paint.

- Paintbrush or sponge.

- Chalk.

Sand the wooden houses so they are smooth and wipe off any loose sawdust. If you want to paint the sides of the houses, do this first, giving the paint plenty of time to dry before proceeding. Paint the flat surfaces of the houses with at least two coats of chalkboard paint, allowing the paint to dry thoroughly between each coat.

When all the paint is dry, use colored chalk to draw in windows, doors, and other details.

Craft Stick Jewelry Box

You can do all sorts of things with wooden craft sticks. This project will give you a nice jewelry box.

You will need:

- Craft sticks.

- Craft knife.

- Wood glue or hot glue.

- 1 felt square.

- Scissors.

- Several buttons.

Make a square with the craft sticks sitting side by side, vertically. Put glue all along another stick and place it horizontally, inset about a half inch from the edge, to hold the square together. Do the same on the other side.

Over this square, make a square with the craft sticks overlapping their edges in a clockwise manner, gluing at the ends. Build up the four sides as high as you like. It will look like log cabin walls. To make the lid of the box do the same as with the bottom. The two horizontal sticks holding the square together will be the inside of the lid. Turn the lid right side up and glue several buttons on top of one another in the center for a handle. Cut a square of felt to fit the inside bottom of the box and glue it in.

Craft Stick Potpourri Box

Follow the instructions for building the jewelry box. However, do not place the felt square inside. Refer to Chapter 5 for instructions on making potpourri to use inside this box.

Crafting With Wooden Cutouts

There are so many things you can do with simple wooden cutouts that I can only mention a few more, hoping that they will spark other crafty ideas:

- Glue nursery rhyme cutouts to the headboard of a crib or toddler bed.

- Glue pretty flower cutouts to the headboard of any bed.

- Glue a finished cutout to the back of a wooden chair or onto the top of a stool.

- Attach them to ornament wooden chests.

- Glue them to the back of a bench.

- Add them to enhance picture frames.

These are just a few of the many ways you can use wooden cutouts to enhance your life. In each case you can use wood glue or hot glue to attach the cutouts.

Cutting Board

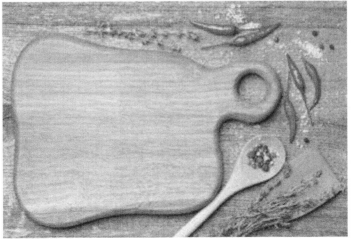

Make your own wooden cutting board.

Always use untreated wood when making a cutting board. You want to avoid leaching chemicals from the wood into your food.

You will need:

- Untreated hardwood – Oak is best – from a half inch to one inch thick and as big as you want it.

- Circular saw.

- Sandpaper – medium grit.

- Food grade mineral oil (also known as cutting board or butcher block oil).

- Clean cotton cloth.

Cut the wood to the desired size and shape. Wipe the board free of any dust or debris. Sand the edges until they are smooth and wipe it clean. Liberally apply the mineral oil and use the clean cloth to rub it into the wood. Wipe in the direction of the grain. Let it dry before turning the board over and oiling the opposite side. Repeat the oiling process four more times, letting the oil soak in well.

To care for your cutting board, do not immerse it in water and never put it in the dishwasher; both of these actions will remove the necessary oils from the wood and may cause the wood to crack. Hand-wash your cutting board and apply additional mineral oil every three to six months.

Decorated Wooden Letters

Wooden letters make a rustic sign

I have some wooden letters on my kitchen wall that spell out "EAT." They're painted in a bright red and embellished with tiny white polka dots.

You can decorate wooden letters and to mark your initials or those of your children. They can enhance the walls of bedrooms or offices.

Individual letters can serve many decorative and practical purposes.

You can do all sorts of things to decorate wooden letters; you don't have to limit yourself to painting them, although they look very nice painted. You can Mod Podge napkins, scrapbook paper, or tissue paper onto them.

When you're finished with your embellishments, attach a bar bracket to the back and hang your letters on the wall.

Decorative Checkerboard

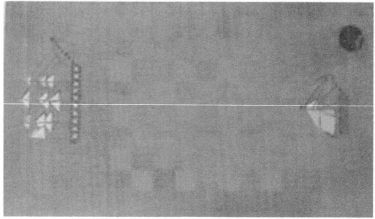

A painted wooden checkerboard

Here you use your painting skills to create a colorful game board. You can also decorate checkers themselves if you wish, although I haven't included these instructions in this project description.

You will need:

- A piece of wood, at least 16 by 16 inches square, and about one inch thick.

- Sandpaper.

- Painter's tape.

- Pencil and ruler.

- Acrylic paint in two contrasting colors (optional third color for outlining squares).

- Brush or foam paint stick.

- Clear acrylic spray.

- Black and white buttons to serve as playing pieces, along with a storage bag or other container.

Sand the wooden square, smoothing the edges and the flat surface. Wipe all surfaces clean. If you don't want to use the natural wood as one of the two square colors, you can paint the entire board a single solid color. Of your two chosen colors, you'll want to use the lighter shade for this. Allow the paint to dry completely before proceeding; if necessary, give it a second coat of paint to ensure even coverage.

Use a pencil and ruler to outline two-inch squares across the checkerboard. Following the penciled outline, carefully paint alternating squares in the second color to complete the checkerboard playing area. If necessary, apply a second coat of paint.

You can end matters here, if you wish. If you want to define the playing area further, use painter's tape to mark a straight line around the outside of the playing area. Select a very dark color (black works best) and paint a narrow line, following your painter's tape, around the outside of the board.

When the paint is dry, remove the tape and lay down fresh tape along each of the horizontal lines on the board. Paint these lines and wait for the paint to dry. Then remove the tape and lay down fresh painter's tape to mark the vertical lines and paint these as well. When the paint is dry and you remove the tape, you will have a beautiful checkerboard with crisply outlined playing squares.

To guard against wear and tear, apply a protective layer of clear acrylic spray. Collect some black and white buttons, put them in a bag or other storage container, and use them as playing pieces.

Front Door Welcome Hanger

This project will give you a unique sign for your front door; you'll be able to welcome visitors in style. These are made from precut wooden cutouts or ornaments found at a local craft store. If you are not into painting, you can often find pre-painted versions that will serve just as effectively.

You will need:

- Thin wood cutouts.

- Acrylic paint.

- Paintbrushes and sponges.

- Nail and hammer with block of wood.

- Wire.

- Clear acrylic spray.

Paint the wooden cutouts however you wish. When the paint is dry, use a nail and hammer over a block of scrap wood to poke holes into the top and both sides of the cutout. Insert a length of wire through each hole and twist it to create a large loop that will hang on a hook or nail on the door. Seal everything with clear acrylic spray to protect your creation from the elements.

Hexagonal Basket

This basket is made with craft sticks and cardboard or poster board. Make the basket as tall or as short as you wish.

You will need:

- Craft sticks.

- Cardboard or poster board.

- Pencil and ruler.

- Wood glue or hot glue.

This uses the same method as the jewelry box to create a different shape. Craft sticks are about four and a half inches long, so cut a hexagonal bottom out of cardboard or poster board. You'll want each side of the hexagon to be four and three quarter inches long.

You will glue the craft sticks along the edges of the hexagon, going around and overlapping the edges of your sticks. You can set a piece of felt in the bottom if desired. Keep gluing until your basket is as tall as you want it to be.

Fairy Door

For a touch of whimsy, make a fairy door and attach it to the bottom of a baseboard with tacky strips.

You will need:

- 9 regular craft sticks.

- Glue and glue gun.

- Craft knife.

- Emery board.

- Large bead.

- Paint.

- Paintbrush.

- Clear acrylic spray.

Line up seven craft sticks close together side by side vertically. Place another one about a half inch from the top horizontally across all seven sticks and glue it. Do the same on the bottom with the ninth stick. When the glue is dry, cut the cross-sticks with a craft knife to fit and sand the edges with an emery board to make them smooth. Turn the door around to face the smooth side. Paint the door as you wish. You can paint a window if you like, hinges, and a doorknocker. Let the paint dry and glue the bead on as a knob. Protect everything with a coat of clear acrylic spray.

Jewelry Holder

Use either antique or new drawer knobs to hang jewelry.

You will need:

- A board about three-quarters to one inch thick, of any length you choose.

- Pencil and ruler.

- Drill and drill bit to fit knob rods.

- Sandpaper.

- Paint or varnish and paintbrush.

- Knobs.

- Screws.

- Wire and wire cutters.

Take a ruler and pencil and evenly space out where you want to install the knobs on the board. It will depend on the size of the knobs, the length of your board, and how many knobs you plan to use. I've found that spacing the knobs one and a half to two inches apart works well for me. You will install the knobs along the center of your board. Drill holes using the appropriate bit for the knob rods at pencil marks. Sand the board down until smooth and wipe it clean. Paint this and let it dry completely before proceeding. If necessary, give the wood a second coat of paint.

Next, you want to make a hanger for your jewelry holder. Turn the board on edge and place two screws in the middle of this edge, one near the left end and the other near the right. Do not screw these all the way in…yet. Cut a piece of wire a little longer than the space between the two screws and twist one end around the first screw head before screwing it down tightly. Take the other end of the wire and repeat this process with the other screw. This wire will suspend the board from a nail on the wall. Install the knobs, hang the board on the wall, and drape your necklaces and bracelets over the knobs.

Lost Sock Holder

I love this craft item and have also discovered that people love to receive this as a gift. It is designed to hang on the wall of your laundry room, where it will help you keep track of your socks.

You will need:

- Piece of wood three quarters of an inch thick, 11 inches long, and 10 inches wide.

- Sandpaper.

- Paint (I use interior latex house paint).

- Paintbrush or sponge.

- Hot glue and glue gun.

- Several wooden alligator-type clothespins.

- Acrylic paint or self-sticking letters.

- Picture hanging bar.

Sand the wood until it is smooth (it doesn't have to be perfect for this craft). Wipe down and paint all surfaces. You can use any color of paint; I painted mine white to match my washer and drier.

Glue the clothespins to the bottom of the dried board lengthwise so that the flat part of the clothespin is glued to the board and the clip area is at the bottom of the board. Space them out evenly. I used four clothespins. If you want, you can paint the clothespins the same color as the board. At the top of the board, letter out the phrase, "Socks Seeking Mates" in acrylic paint or with the stick-on letters. Glue a picture-hanging bar to the center top back and hang it in the laundry room where it'll be easy to see and use. If you clip those unmatched socks to the clothespins, they will easy to reach when the mate appears.

Miniature Village

Little villages are quite popular in some circles; now you can make your own out of wood. Craft stores usually carry small blocks of wood shaped like various buildings. Some are flat-roofed and up to one and a half inch thick, while others will just look like blocks of wood with a roof on top. In this project, you'll use paint to turn these nondescript blocks of wood into your own miniature village.

You will need:

- House cutouts or blocks.

- Sandpaper.

- Acrylic paint.

- Paintbrush.

Sand the houses until they are completely smooth, including the corners. Wipe down the wood, and then you're ready to start painting. After painting a base coat for the walls and another color for the roof, you can add the details that will make your village unique. Add windows, doors, shutters, addresses, a front porch, trees, shrubs, and flower boxes brimming with flowers.

Pallet Headboard

Wooden pallets can be repurposed for both artistic and practical use.

There are many ways to make a headboard out of pallets, but this is my favorite. I like the rustic look, so I just sand the pallet down so it can't hurt anything and leave it looking natural.

You will need:

- pallets (the ones with the slats close together are nice, but hard to get hold of. Just use the regular ones if you can't find the others).

- Sandpaper.

- two-by-fours cut the length of the pallets set side by side.

- Anchor screws.

- Drill.

When you go to select your pallets, look for a stamp inside a square that reads "HT.". This stamp means the wood was heat-treated instead of chemically processed. I don't think you really want chemically treated pallets emitting fumes close to where you lay your head at night.

Sand the pallets so that rough spots will not be a problem. You can wood burn designs into the pallets, paint them, or stain them, using any colors or designs you want. You can even leave them plain if you prefer the natural look.

Screw the two-by-fours into the wall at the baseboard level just behind the head of the bed. Anchor them well; pallets are very heavy and the two-by-fours will be supporting all of their weight. Set the pallets on the two-by-four ledge and screw them into the wall toward the top.

Pallet Wall Hanging

Pallets are heavy and you need to use the same two-by-four trick here as for the headboard project when you hang them on the wall. Sand down the pallet and then either wood burn a design or paint one, then hang it on the wall. One friend painted each slat a different color, but left one untouched. The resulting art looks lovely on her wall.

Pallet Flag

Pallet art looks good, indoors or outside.

These are often hung on the side of a garage or barn as well as indoors. You will need to find a pallet where the slats are close together for this craft. Use exterior paint if you plan to hang it outside. Once again, use the two-by-four method of hanging for safe results.

You will need:

- 1 pallet with slats close together.

- Paint in shades of red, white, and blue.

- Paintbrush.

- Wide painter's tape.

- Pencil and ruler.

Before you start painting, sand down any rough spots on the face of the pallet. Use your pencil and ruler to draw a square in the upper left corner proportionate to the rest of the flag. The size will depend your preference and on the size of the pallet. This square will be the area for the stars. Start by outlining the square with painter's tape. Paint the square white and let it dry. Cut star shapes out of painter's tape. I found it easy to make a star-shaped template using a piece of poster board; I then drew around the template along the painter's tape, then cut out as many painter's tape stars as would fit in the square.

Affix the painter's tape stars in the white square. Paint over the square with blue and let the paint dry. If necessary, give it a second coat. Once the paint has dried, remove the painter's tape and you will have a star-studded blue patch.

Paint the rest of the pallet slats alternating red and white. Again, if needed, give them a second coat of paint. Once the paint is dry, you can hang your patriotic flag for all to salute.

Pine Coasters

For this craft, you will need a circular saw to cut thin blocks of pine.

You will need:

- Saw.

- Pine that can be cut into three-by-three-inch squares between a half inch and one inch thick.

- Sandpaper.

- Mineral oil.

- Cloth.

- Stick-on felt pads.

Cut the pine in the dimensions described above and use sandpaper to smooth the edges and surface of each coaster. With a soft cloth, rub some mineral oil into the top side with a cloth and let it dry. This will prevent the pine from staining. Attach four felt pads to the bottom of the coaster, near the outer edges.

Pine Hot Pads

Make these in the same way as with the coasters, only cut them into five-by-five-inch blocks that are one inch thick. Sand these just as you did with the coasters, then coat the top surface with mineral oil and add felt pads to the bottom.

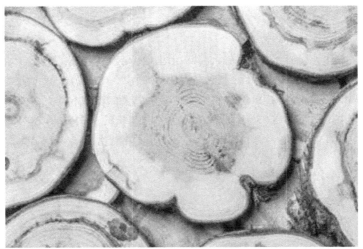

Use the cross-section of trees for natural heat absorption.

Scrap Wood Wall Art

Some hardware stores have a big bin where they throw scrap wood. Sometimes you can get nice pieces there for next to nothing or even free. Pick through the scrap wood and take pieces that are straight and not too damaged.

There are many things you can do with scrap wood. You can use a wood burner and write a phrase, a name or a design into the wood. You can paint on the wood or stencil something onto it. You'll often use long boards for the display side of your wall art and keep smaller but sturdy smaller pieces to reinforce your board, to fasten several boards together, or to create depth by adding thickness to your display piece.

You can nail or screw several boards onto a vertical piece. Attach a wire with two screws to the back of your board and you will instantly have some wall art. I prefer the rustic look, so splintered and rough weathered pieces don't bother me. Just be careful when working with them to avoid getting splinters in your fingers.

Storage Crates

You can usually find ready-made wood storage crates in a craft shop or hardware store. These crates have a wooden frame and wooden slats along the sides. Use these to store children's toys or to stash magazines next to your couch for easy access. They also make great magazine and newspaper racks.

- **You will need:**

- Storage crate.

- Sandpaper.

- Interior house paint.

- Paintbrush.

- Painted wooden ornaments (optional).

- Hot glue and glue gun.

- Clear acrylic spray.

Crates Just Asking To Be Decorated

Sand down the storage crates until they are smooth, then wipe them clean of sawdust. Use house paint and a brush to paint the crates. I like to paint the inside one color and the outside another. I have also painted each slat a different color at times, but you can do whatever you like.

Let the paint dry completely before proceeding. Purchase some plain flat wooden ornaments from the craft store. Paint them yourself or buy them pre-painted. Glue them to the crate using the glue gun, arranging them across the slats. I have used wooden initials of my child and used it for toy storage, but I'm sure you can think up plenty of other practical applications. When you're finished, seal everything with a clear acrylic spray.

Wall Coat Rack

This is a rustic kind of coat rack but I really like the look of it. You can leave the wood plain or decorate it with paint or a wood burned design, whatever you want.

You will need:

- 3 boards, all the same width and length and about one to one and a half inch thick.

- Boards of any thickness to hold them together .

- Screws.

- Drill.

- Metal hooks with screws to install them.

My boards were about four inches wide and I allowed a five-inch gap between them. Screw the vertical board into the other two boards, one at each end about two inches down from the top with gaps in between. Mine came out about 30 inches wide when I was done. Install the hooks on the three boards. Center them on the boards. Decorate this coat rack as desired and screw it into the wall, using anchor screws at the top of each side.

Walking Stick

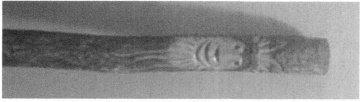

Carved walking sticks are useful as well as ornamental.

Walking sticks are fun to make. You want to start out with a fresh branch that you cut off a tree. Live wood is softer and will be much easier to work than deadwood.

You will need:

- A branch up to two inches thick at the large end and 55 to 65 inches tall.

- A three-quarter inch diameter copper water pipe cut about one inch long.

- Quick-drying epoxy glue.

- Small saw.

- Sharp knife.

- Wood burning set (optional).

- Clear acrylic spray.

Cut the branch from the tree and remove any side branches. Trim the top and bottom carefully to avoid splintering the wood. Use your knife to whittle away the bark. The light-colored wood just beneath the bark is what you want to see.

You can carve two eyes, a nose and mouth at the head or top of the walking stick to add a touch of whimsy or you may carve or burn ornamental designs.

To keep the bottom from splintering, whittle it down to fit within the copper pipe. Put epoxy on this section and insert it into the copper pipe. Let the glue dry before using the cane. Let the stick cure and dry for about one month before applying any shellac or stain. When you're finished working over your cane, seal the wood with a coat of clear acrylic.

Wood Burned Coasters And Hot Pads

Wood burner In Action

You will need:

- Round or square flat pieces of wood about three by three inches for coasters and five by five for hot pads.

- Wood burning tool and tip.

- Pencil.

- Mineral oil.

Draw a design on the flat surface of the coaster or hot pad with a pencil. Use the wood burner to burn the design into the wood. Let everything cool down and rub the surface with mineral oil.

Wood Burned Picture Frame

A wood burner is an electric tool that generates enough heat at its tip to actually char wood. A variety of shaped tips can be attached to provide differing textures to your wood burning. The best woods to use for wood burning projects are soft, like basswood.

You will need:

- Wood burning tool and metal tips.

- Soft wood picture frame.

- Pencil.

- Sandpaper.

- Stain.

Draw a design on a wooden frame with a pencil or use transfer paper to copy a pattern. Burn the design into the wood, following these guidelines. When you are finished, you can sand down any rough surfaces, then use a light-colored stain to enhance the appearance, if you wish.

Chapter 7: Sculpting and Modeling

Working with clay is something most of us have done when we were very little. Play dough has been around for years and provides children with one of their first experiences with sculpting.

Sculpting ranges from making pottery and forming likenesses of animals and people to making jewelry. You can do so many things with clay that the possibilities can be overwhelming. This chapter should help you organize all those possibilities and let you get started. As you grow in experience, you will get a feel for which clays work best for certain projects and you'll find it easier to get started.

Types Of Clay

Polymer clay is colorful and easy to work with.

Polymer clay is very popular today. It comes in little rectangles wrapped in plastic and is available in a variety of colors. It is made of PVC and needs to be kneaded or flattened with a pasta maker (which should never be used for anything else, a tool dedicated to clay work, never for use with food) to make it pliable. Some people put their polymer clay in a food processor to break it down, too.

The finished product is then air dried or baked in an oven. Unused polymer clay should be stored in a cool dark place. If it becomes too hard, you can soak it in warm water for about 20 minutes before using.

Polymer clay contains pigments that can transfer to the surface on which you are working. For this reason, I work my clay on a flat plastic cutting board to keep the pigment from staining my table. The fun thing about polymer clay is that you can blend colors together completely or make swirly patterns or mosaic-like patterns just by cutting, rolling, twisting, and otherwise manipulating the clay.

To work with this clay you will need a pasta machine, slicing blades, a rolling pin, and toothpicks. You also need parchment paper on which to place the clay when you bake it. If you find it hard to keep fingerprints off the clay, cover your hands with latex gloves. To preserve your work, you can use a glaze designed specifically for polymer clay or you can just spray it with clear acrylic.

Air-dry clay is found in craft stores. True to its name, you don't have to bake this type of clay or fire it in a kiln. Most air-dry clays are non-toxic and very inexpensive. They usually can be painted when dry. The only real problem with air-drying clay is that it tends to crack and flake over time and you won't want to get it wet – water can destroy it entirely.

Natural earth clay is made from the substance that comes from the earth. It is usually reddish brown in color but may have pigment added to make it appear darker. It must remain moist while you work it, making this clay a challenge to work with. If the clay dries, it is no good. Most pottery is made from earth clay. This natural clay also requires firing in a kiln, where the temperatures are much higher than a regular oven.

Salt clay is what many teachers use in elementary school because it is easily created and is very inexpensive. Salt maps are made from this type of clay, which is sometimes referred to as salt dough. My family has made Christmas ornaments from salt clay, adding some cinnamon to give off a holiday scent.

The recipe is as follows:

Stir together one cup salt and two cups flour in a large mixing bowl. Gradually add in three-quarters of a cup of cold water and mix it to a doughy consistency. If you want to add food coloring, pour the coloring in the water and add it that way.

Salt dough can be hardened in an oven at a temperature of 180 degrees Fahrenheit. The time required for hardening depends on the thickness of the objects. When completely hardened, the object should feel hard to the touch, but it should not be overly brown. Salt dough can also be air-dried.

Paper mache clay is also very easy to make. It is lightweight, making it perfect for larger projects. It air dries well and is paintable, but you should avoid getting the finished project wet.

To make paper mache clay you need a roll of toilet paper. Put roll and all in a large bowl and pour warm water on top of it. The cardboard tube should slide out easily when the paper is wet. Remove the roll from the water and wring out as much moisture as you can. Break the toilet paper into small chunks and set them aside on a tray. In another bowl combine three-quarters of a cup of school glue, one cup of flour, and one cup of joint compound, commonly available in hardware stores. Add in the paper, creating a mixture that will be sticky and fibrous. Mix well and store in a re-closeable plastic bag for up to one week. This clay is perfect for spreading over a base to make various shapes.

Baking soda clay is another homemade clay that is easy to make and use. It is very smooth and is pure white in color.

To make baking soda clay, combine one cup of cornstarch, two cups of baking soda and 1-1/4 cups of cold water in a non-stick saucepan. Use a wooden spoon to stir this mixture until smooth, then cook it over medium low heat, stirring constantly. When the mixture takes on the consistency of mashed potatoes, remove the pot from the heat. Let the mixture cool for five minutes, then transfer it into a bowl and cover it with a moist towel.

When the mixture has cooled to room temperature, it is ready to use. If the clay starts to dry out, sprinkle a little water on the surface and knead it in. You should use baking soda clay right away because it dries out quickly. Shaped objects will dry in about two days if left to air dry, depending on the size. You can also bake baking soda clay objects at 150 degrees Fahrenheit, with the oven door cracked open. Check after 20 minutes and then every 10 minutes to prevent browning.

Clay Projects

Air-Drying Clay Tealight Holder

These holders are low-sided. The tealights fit perfectly inside, allowing the light to shine clearly. These delightful holders will add ambiance to your bathroom and romantic lighting anywhere in your home. Commercial air-drying clay is best, but you can use baking soda clay or salt clay for this project.

You will need:

- Air-drying clay.

- Tea lights.

- Butter knife.

- Water.

- Fine sandpaper.

Roll a handful of clay into a ball that's a little larger than the tea light. Take the tea light and press it into the center of the ball so that the clay comes up the sides but the candle doesn't press through the bottom. Wiggle the tea light to slightly enlarge the depression so you can easily insert and remove it. Keeping the tea light in the hole, gently reshape the clay into a round ball. Without otherwise misshaping the ball, carefully cut off the bottom to create a flat base, but avoid cutting into the candle.

You can mark geometric shapes or patterns on the clay with a knife or pointed stick, or you can leave it smooth. To smooth the clay, use a little water on your fingers. When you are finished working on the candleholder, remove the tea light and let the piece dry for 48 hours. Use sandpaper lightly to smooth any rough edges.

Architectural Designs

Cornices and other ornaments are easily made using paper mache.

Adding architectural designs to a picture frame, a doorframe, a headboard, or other piece of furniture is easy using paper mache clay. This medium is very light so it won't add significant weight to any structure. You can find plenty of ideas in books of architectural structures or by wandering through older downtown buildings. Then it's easy enough to replicate them using paper mache clay spread over card stock as a framework. Let it dry and treat it with varnish or paint, then glue it to the wall or furniture you wish to enhance. People will never know it is just some cheap clay you created in your kitchen.

Baking Soda Clay Pressed-Flower Hangings

Pressed flowers bring nature indoors year round.

Add a few drops of essential oils to the mix when you are making the baking soda clay. This will scent the room when the sun hits the window hanger. This clay is pure white, providing a striking background for the pressed flowers.

You will need:

- Baking soda clay.

- Wax paper.

- Rolling pin.

- Round cookie cutters.

- Skewer.

- Parchment paper and baking sheet.

- Pressed flowers or leaves.

- Mod Podge.

- Paintbrush.

- Ribbon or string.

Roll out your baking soda clay on wax paper until it is a quarter inch thick. Cut out rounds, ovals, or any other shape with cookie cutters. Poke a hole near the top with a skewer to allow you to hang it later. Set these pieces on a parchment-covered cookie sheet and let them air dry for two days or bake them in a 150-degree Fahrenheit oven with the door cracked open until the clay is hard and dry.

Let the rounds cool to room temperature. Paint the front with a layer of Mod Podge. Place pressed flowers or leaves on top of the wet Mod Podge and gently paint over them with another layer of Mod Podge. Let these dry completely, then run the ribbon or string through the hole, tie it to make a loop, and hang it up.

Clay-Covered Jars

These little colorful jars are wonderful for storing change, paper clips, tacks, twist ties, rubber bands, and even candy.

You will need:

- Pint canning jars with rim and lid (alternative: use baby food jars).

- Polymer clay.

- Wax paper.

- Parchment paper and baking sheet with sides.

Tear off pieces of clay and stick them onto the jar. Make sure none of the jar shows through and stop adding clay before you reach the threading for the lid.

Roll the jar on wax paper to help merge the clay together. Line a cookie sheet with parchment paper. Place your jars, upside down, on this cookie sheet. Slide the cookie sheet into a 275-degree Fahrenheit oven for 20 minutes. Turn off the oven and let the jars cool to room temperature before removing them. Add the lids to your jars and they're ready to be used.

Clay-Covered Thumbtacks

You need the flat type of thumbtack to make this project. The coverings are made separately and glued onto the thumbtack after being baked and cured.

You will need:

- Polymer clay.

- Thumbtacks.

- Scrap of wood or piece of foam core.

- Parchment paper and baking sheet.

- E6000 craft glue.

Press your thumbtacks partway into a piece of scrap wood or a piece of foam core, anything that will hold them steady. Condition the clay until it is soft and pliable. For each thumbtack, tear off a pea-sized chunk of clay and shape it into a ball. Place this against the tack head and gently press downward to conform the ball to the shape of the tack head. Set the clay dot on parchment paper with the flat side down and bake at 275 degrees Fahrenheit for 20 to 45 minutes, depending on how thick you made the dot. Let it cool to room temperature. Place a drop of E6000 glue on the head of the tack, fit the flat side of the dot against the glue, and press down. Let the tack dry for 12 hours before moving it.

Colored And Waxed Salt Clay Hangers

You can color salt dough in vibrant shades. I make hearts for Valentine's Day and they are always a big hit. These keep a long time because they are protected by the wax.

You will need:

- Wax paper.

- A reclosable plastic bag.

- Salt clay.

- Cookie cutters.

- Acrylic paint.

- Paintbrush.

- Flour (optional).

- Skewer.

- Baking sheet covered with parchment paper.

- Ribbon or string.

- Paraffin wax.

- Large empty metal can, washed.

- Electric skillet with high sides or a saucepan.

- Christmas tree ornament hooks.

- More wax paper and something to hang the ornament from to dry.

Put some salt clay in the re-closeable plastic bag. Add a few drops of red or pink acrylic paint, close the bag and squish it around in your hands, mixing the paint into the clay. If the clay starts to get too soft, add quarter-teaspoonfuls of flour at a time until it becomes more firm. Add enough paint to saturate the clay and give it a vibrant color.

Place some wax paper on your work surface to prevent the clay from staining it. Cover the clay with another piece of wax paper to keep it from staining the rolling pin. Roll this out until it is a quarter inch thick. Cut out heart shapes with the cookie cutter. Use the skewer to make holes in the top of the humps of each heart. Bake or air dry your shapes. I usually let them air dry for a couple of days.

Because they are already colored, you don't really need to do any painting. You can embellish them, however with polka dots or by outlining the edges. Let the paint dry completely before proceeding.

Place the paraffin in the can. Set the can on an electric skillet or in a saucepan; add water to the pan, being careful that none of it gets into the paraffin. You will need enough paraffin to cover your ornament when it is dipped.

Once the paraffin is melted, pull the string through the skewer hole and attach a Christmas tree ornament hook to it, bending the bottom to secure the string. Dip the ornament in the paraffin so that it covers completely. Lift it out. Dip it a second time. Lift it out and let the excess wax drip off. Hang the ornament to cool. Once the ornament is completely dry, smooth any rough edges by cutting off excess wax. Then, using a cotton swab dipped in boiling water, seal the paraffin edges again.

Crochet Hook Covers

A Crochet Hook Grip Made Of Polymer Clay

These cover a commercial metal crochet hook. It not only looks attractive, but it makes them easier to handle if your hands are stiff or your skin is sensitive.

You will need:

- Metal crochet hook.

- Polymer clay, three to five colors.

- Butter knife.

- Parchment paper and baking sheet.

- Permanent marker.

Make logs of three to five colors about two inches long. Twist the logs together. Five colors are possible, but for small hooks only use three or the cover will be too big and bulky. Roll and twist the clay until the log is smooth and about four inches long. Gently poke the flat end of the hook into the end of the clay log and carefully push it down the shank until just before the flat area that gives the size of the hook. Roll the clay-encased hook to smooth it and taper the clay as it approaches the hook. Tap the end of the clay on the table to flatten it. Take a small ball of white polymer clay, attach it to the top like a cap, and flatten it down. You will later write the size of the hook on it with a permanent marker.

Place hook and all on parchment paper on a cookie sheet and bake at 275 degrees Fahrenheit for 15 minutes. Let the hook cool to room temperature before you move it.

Colored Pencil Holder

I love to draw with colored pencils; they aren't just for children. This pencil holder will make it easy to select the color you need

You will need:

- Air-drying clay.

- Colored pencils.

- Acrylic paint.

- Paintbrush.

- Butter knife.

Roll a large piece of clay into a ball that is large enough to accommodate 12 holes for 12 pencils. Flatten the ball on the bottom to make a stable base. Push the unsharpened end of the colored pencils into the clay, being careful not to disturb any existing holes, but going deep enough that the pencils will stay seated in the holder. The finished product will look somewhat like a porcupine, with all the colored pencils sticking out of it.

Wiggle each pencil to enlarge the hole slightly so that it'll be easy to slide the pencils in and out. Remove the pencils and clean off their ends. Let the piece dry overnight. The next day, even though the clay is not completely dry, you can carefully smooth out any rough spots.

Let this project dry for two or three days. Once it is completely dry, you can paint it with acrylics, being careful not to get paint in the pencil holes. When the paint is dry, put your pencils in the holes and voila, you have a practical and beautiful place to store your colored pencils.

Country Window Hanger

Form your salt clay ornaments into any flat shape you want and cut a hole in the middle. Poke a couple small holes toward the top to accommodate the hanger. Instead of a photo, cover the center hole with pretty scrapbook paper or tissue paper the light can shine through. Use a length of pretty satin ribbon threaded through the hanging holes and tied off in the back to suspend in the middle of a window.

Decorative Mask

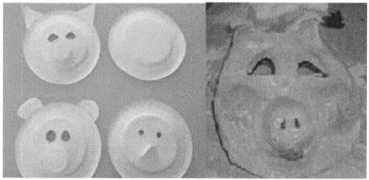

L: Preparation – (clockwise from Upper Right): Plain plate, bird, pig, cat (or dog); R: Finished Product.

Masks are very popular wall hangings. You can make a theater mask, a masquerade face-covering, or an African style mask by using paper mache clay and a paper plate.

You will need:

- Paper mache clay.

- Paper plate (not plastic).

- Scissors.

- Plastic wrap.

- Butter knife.

- Acrylic paint and brush.

- Clear acrylic spray.

Cut the plate to the shape of the mask you want to make, then cut out eye holes. You can build up a nose use masking tape and cardstock, if you want. You can do the same with the lips.

Cover the mask with a thin coat of clay, spreading it with a butter knife. Let the outside of the mask dry completely before turning over the mask and adding clay to the inside and letting it dry.

Paint as desired and when dry, spray with clear acrylic spray to protect it. I've made beautiful and colorful sugar skull masks using this method.

Paper Mache Clay Butterfly

In this project, you will spread the paper mache over cardstock to make a colorful butterfly that can be hung, since this clay is very light.

You will need:

- Paper mache clay.

- Scissors.

- Pencil.

- Cardstock.

- Aluminum foil.

- Masking tape.

- Plastic wrap.

- Butter knife.

- Craft knife.

- Emery board.

- Acrylic paint/brush.

- Permanent markers.

Draw a large butterfly on the cardstock and cut it out. Bend the wings slightly upward. Roll a piece of aluminum foil into a log for the body and attach it to the underside of the paper butterfly wings with thin strips of masking tape. Cover the foil completely because the clay will stick to the tape and not the foil.

Lay a large square of plastic wrap on a table and place the butterfly, upside down, on top. Spread paper mache clay with a butter knife on the underside of the wings and then cover the body as well. Cover all the edges, all surfaces of the cardstock wings and all the masking tape that covers the foil on the underside. Fold the plastic wrap over the clay and smooth it by rubbing along the plastic with the flat part of the knife. Set your butterfly over a bowl to dry. Flip the butterfly over and do the same to the top side of the butterfly, using more paper mache clay.

Once everything is completely dry, remove any excess clay from the edges of the wings with a sharp craft knife and smooth the edges with an emery board. Paint the body a dark color and then paint the wings with acrylic paint. Use permanent markers to outline the wings and mark veins. You can attach a nylon line to the center of the butterfly and hang it, attach it to a wall, or just set it on a table.

Paper Mache Village

You can make an entire community with just some milk cartons, and paper mache.

You will need:

- Milk cartons.

- Card stock.

- Paper mache clay.

- Masking tape.

- Acrylic paint and brushes.

- Dried moss.

- Silk or dried flowers.

- Glue and glue gun.

Use clean milk cartons and cardstock to build a framework for houses and other buildings. If you need to tape something together to make the framework, use masking tape because paper mache clay will stick to it.

Spread clay over the cartons or forms and let it dry. Paint each building as you wish. Add silk or dried flowers to window boxes or near the ground and glue moss growing up the roof, down the sides, or along the base of the buildings to suggest grass.

Polymer Clay Covered Cans

Use these imaginative containers to hold pencils, utensils, coins, paper clips, or anything else you can think of. Decorate them as you wish.

You will need:

- Cans.

- Polymer clay.

- Butter knife.

- Sandpaper.

- Acrylic paint (optional).

- Clear acrylic spray.

Remove labels from the empty cans and clean them well. Condition the clay and roll it into small, long coils. Start at the bottom of the can, coiling the clay around it and leaving no spaces between layers of clay. Once the can is covered from bottom to top, use the butter knife to smooth the sides of the can by pressing and spreading the clay. Decorate your can with additional polymer clay if you like. Let everything dry for 48 hours, sand any rough spots, and decorate with paint if you like.

I made jack-o-lanterns for Halloween using this method, coiling orange clay and smoothing it. I then cut black triangles for eyes and nose and a toothy black grin for a mouth and attached them to the orange "face."

Polymer Clay Cupboard Knobs

Ceramic Door Knobs

160

You will be covering existing knobs with polymer clay. Make sure to get metal or ceramic knobs that can tolerate the heat of an oven. You can find plenty of used knobs at garage sales, second hand stores, and flea markets.

You will need:

- Polymer sheets.

- Pasta machine.

- Knife.

- Ruler.

Remove all other hardware from the knob, including screws. You only want the knob and the rod that goes through the door. Run the polymer clay through your pasta machine a few times. Cut a circle of clay that is a little larger than the knob and place the knob face down on this circle. Lift the sides of the clay up and over the knob, covering it entirely. Smooth the clay gently to get rid of any bubbles or ripples.

Cut a strip of clay about three inches long and a half inch wide and wrap that around the stem of the knob. Your knob should look like a fat mushroom at this point. Note: you can form the clay into different shapes, if you want to do more than just follow the shape of the knob.

Cure the clay by placing it in an oven for 20 minutes at 275 degrees Fahrenheit. After cooling the knob to room temperature, you can insert the rod, screw it in, and install the knob on your cupboard door.

Polymer Clay Coasters

These can be made in a single color or you can swirl and mix your clay to make colorful designs.

You will need:

- Polymer clay.

- Pasta machine.

- Knife.

- Ruler.

- Felt pads.

- Glue.

- Clear acrylic spray or Mod Podge.

Roll the clay out until it is a quarter inch thick. Cut out three-by-three-inch squares or similar-sized circles. Let these air dry. I would not suggest baking it because this will cause the clay to warp and not lay flat.

Once it is dry, glue felt pads onto the bottom. To protect the top surface, spray it with clear acrylic or brush it with Mod Podge.

Polymer Clay Garden Markers

Polymer clay isn't the sturdiest clay in the world, but these garden markers will serve you well indoors, gracing your potted plants. Polymer clay is a form of plastic, so there is no need to protect these markers with a sealant.

You will need:

- Polymer clay that can be oven baked.

- Cookie sheet.

- Parchment paper.

- Rolling pin.

- Butter knife.

- Letter stamps.

Form balls of clay that are an inch and a quarter in diameter. You will need one ball per marker. Roll the ball into a log that is around five and a half inches long and flatten it to a quarter inch thick. The marker should now have the shape of a long rectangle. Use the butter knife to cut one end at an angle, effectively creating a point. Smooth the edges with the flat of the knife, smooth it further with your fingers, and then place the marker on a parchment-lined cookie sheet. Use the letter stamps to spell out plant names on the stakes. Bake the garden markers per package directions.

Polymer Clay Pen Covers

Pen Covers (And Crochet Hook Covers) Made From Polymer Clay

For this project, use clear-barreled pens. You should be able to remove the tip and ink tube; we'll put it back together when we're done. You can use one color or multiple colors to make this project.

You will need:

- Pasta machine.

- Polymer clay.

- Barrel pens.

- Wax paper.

- Parchment paper.

- Cookie sheet.

Remove the caps and the ink tube from the pens and set them aside. Condition and run the clay through the pasta machine, then tear or cut it into small pieces. Stick the pieces, overlapping, on the barrel of the pen up to where the tip screws in and up over the top so that none of the pen shows through. Wrap this in wax paper and roll it to create a smooth surface. You can cover any bare spaces on the pen by exerting a little pressure to squish the clay together.

Place the covered barrels on a parchment-covered baking sheet and bake at 275 degrees Fahrenheit for about 20 minutes. This should not melt the pen barrel. Remove from the oven and let it set until cool. Replace the ink tube and tip.

Polymer Clay Trinket Bowl

These little bowls are useful to hold your rings and bracelets while you're washing the dishes, for corralling spare change, and for a hundred different uses.

You will need:

- Polymer clay.

- Pasta maker.

- Small glass or plastic bowl.

- Knife.

- Clear acrylic spray.

Condition the clay and roll it out to a quarter inch thick. Take an existing cup or bowl and turn it upside down. Centering the sheet of clay, carefully drape it over the bowl or cup. Press the clay down at the top to make it flat. Let the clay dry on the bowl for two hours or until the clay holds its shape when removed from the bowl. Cut off any uneven edges with a knife, set the bowl upright, and let it air dry for 48 hours. Spray all sides with clear acrylic.

Salt Dough Doilies

Take some old fashioned crocheted doilies and turn them into something new and modern. You can set them on a table or shelf or hang them on the wall. You can even paint them with acrylic paint if you like.

You will need:

- Wax paper.

- Salt dough.

- Rolling pin.

- Crocheted doily.

- Knife.

- Skewer.

- String or ribbon (optional).

- Scissors.

Lay some wax paper on your work surface and set your salt dough on top. Roll the dough out with a rolling pin until it is a half inch thick and as large as the size of the doily.

Place the doily on top of the rolled-out salt clay and lightly press down with your hands. Use the rolling pin to gently, but firmly press the doily pattern into the salt dough. Carefully lift off the doily. Trim any uneven edges off the clay with the knife and poke a hole in the top if you want to hang your doily impression.

Let the doily impression dry completely before you flip it over and let the back dry. If you want, you can paint your work of art. When finished, cut a string or ribbon long enough to go through the hole and tie it in a loop to hang.

Salt Clay Pet Print Memorials

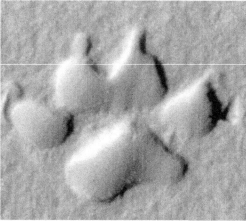

Nontoxic Paw Printing

These pet paw memorials will always remind you of your pet. I use round cookie cutters to create a round shape, which I press my pet's paw into, let it dry, and then decorate it. A friend of mine did these when her cats were kittens and then again when they had grown up. She placed them in a deep glass-covered frame with a picture of the cat along with the prints. Salt dough is nice to use because it doesn't stick to the paws of your pets. Even if a small amount of residue remains, it is completely nontoxic. NOTE: You can also make handprints or footprints of your children by cutting the circles a little larger.

You will need:

- Salt dough.

- Wax paper.

- Rolling pin.

- Round cookie cutter (or glass).

- Skewer.

- Acrylic paints and brush.

- Glitter (optional).

Roll out the salt dough on the wax paper to about a quarter to a half inch thick. Cut circles of the preferred size. Place your pet's paw in the center of the circle and press lightly down to make an impression that presses partway into the dough. With the skewer, poke a hole in the center near the top rim of the circle.

Let the circles dry completely. You can speed the drying process by placing them in the microwave for two minutes, then continuing to heat in 20 second intervals until the project is dry. When the paw prints are thoroughly dried, you can paint the indentation of the paw and shake on some glitter, if you wish, before the paint dries.

Salt Dough Picture Frame

These picture frames make nice gifts for Valentine's day, especially if you make them heart-shaped.

You will need:

- Salt dough.

- A photograph.

- Wax paper.

- Rolling pin.

- Knife.

- Large heart cookie cutter.

- Smaller round cookie cutter that will fit in the middle of the heart.

- Skewer.

- Baking sheet covered with parchment paper.

- Acrylic paint and brush.

- Hot glue.

- String or ribbon.

- Scissors.

Place wax paper on the work surface and roll the salt clay out to about a quarter inch thick. Cut out the hearts then cut a hole in the middle, using the circular cookie cutter. Make a small hole in the center of each hump of the heart near the top. You'll place a string or ribbon through these later to make a hanger. Bake or microwave the salt clay hearts on a cookie sheet covered with parchment paper at 180 degrees Fahrenheit for about a half hour, depending on the thickness. You can also microwave on high for three minutes and then in 10-second intervals until dry.

Paint the heart and let it dry. Trim the photo larger than the hole in the heart but not so big as to extend past the edges of the heart. Glue the photo to the back of the heart. Cut a length of string or ribbon and tie it in a loop through the small hanging holes. If you want a more finished look to the back, you can cut a felt heart slightly smaller than the clay heart and glue it to the back to cover the photograph.

Salt Dough Rainbow

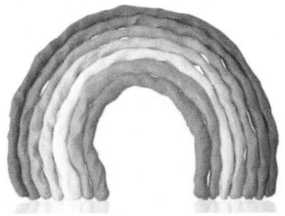

A rainbow will brighten any space.

You can hang this rainbow in a window or on the wall. You will need several colors of salt dough; these are made by adding food coloring when you mix it. For your rainbow you will want salt dough in red, blue, yellow, green, purple and orange.

You will need:

- Multiple colors of salt dough.

- Skewer.

- Wax paper.

- Parchment paper.

- Nylon fishing line or lacy ribbon.

- Scissors.

Roll out the different colors of dough in long coils. Place wax paper on the table and shape one coil into the shape of a wide horseshoe, then lay the other coils beneath this one to create a large multi-colored rainbow. Poke a hanging hole in the very top center of the first coil. Press down on your rainbow so the back will be flat.

Place your rainbow in the microwave on a microwave-safe plate with parchment paper underneath. Microwave on high for three minutes and then in 10-second intervals until the rainbow has dried completely. Let it set in the microwave for five minutes to cool. Put the string or ribbon through the hole and tie it in a loop to hang.

Salt Clay Animals

Add depth to your clay animals by building them in layers.

These animals are flat, designed to hang on large houseplants or over window locks and lamp knobs.

You will need:

- Wax paper.

- Salt clay.

- Rolling pin.

- Animal-shaped cookie cutters.

- Skewer.

- Parchment paper covering a baking sheet or microwaveable dish.

- Acrylic paint and brushes.

- String.

- Scissors.

Roll out the salt clay on wax paper with a rolling pin. Cut out animals with cookie cutters and poke a hole in the top with a skewer to hang. Place the clay animals on a baking sheet or dish covered with parchment and either bake or microwave as above. Once the animals are dry, paint and decorate. Cut a length of string and thread it through the hole, tying in a loop to hang.

Note: Make a three dimensional bird by adding a wing. Stick the wing on before baking.

Stamped Clay Wall Hangings

Cut baking soda clay into rounds, ovals or any other shape and use rubber stamps to impress an image on them. You can wipe paint over the stamped indentation for greater contrast, if you wish. You can use alphabet stamps to imprint initials and then glue glitter into the indentation. The variations are endless!

You will need:

- Baking soda clay.

- Wax paper.

- Rolling pin.

- Cookie cutters or a knife for cutting freehand.

- Skewer.

- Rubber stamps.

- Parchment paper and cookie sheet.

- Acrylic paint and brush.

- Ribbon or string.

Roll out the clay with a rolling pin on wax paper until it is a quarter inch thick. Use a cookie cutter or cut the shape freehand. Press a rubber stamp in the center, then carefully remove it, so that the indentation comes out clean. Place on a parchment-covered cookie sheet and bake or let air dry. Paint or otherwise decorate the indented area, let it dry, and then insert ribbon or string through the hole, tying it in a loop to form a hanger.

Chapter 8: Tape Crafting

Some clever crafters have made prom dresses from duct tape; I find that simply amazing! Some of the crafts in this chapter do use duct tape, although these crafts are not necessarily wearable. You'll discover that duct tape is highly versatile. It now comes in a variety of colors and patterns that go far beyond the original silver. You can even buy page-sized sheets of the stuff now!

Washi tape comes in hundreds of colors and designs.

Another widely used craft tape is washi tape. This is the "masking tape" of Japan. At the request of several Japanese artists, a masking tape manufacturer in Japan came up with a colorful tape and started producing rolls with beautiful patterns and colors. Made of rice paper, washi tape can now be found in most American craft stores.

Washi tape is fun and easy to use. It comes in rolls that are easily dispensed. While it has an adhesive on the back, the tape is easily lifted off and repositioned or reused. This tape can be written on, too.

Some crafts can use either tape interchangeably. However, if you really need your craft to hold together, "stick" with duct tape. It's much more durable and it's water-resistant.

Duct Tape Bookmark

Duct tape bookmarks are quite durable. They slip onto the corners of your pages so they will never stress the binding. You can make these out of washi tape too, although duct tape is more durable and will stay in place easier.

You will need:

- Cardstock.

- Ruler.

- Pencil.

- Scissors.

- Duct tape.

On cardstock, mark off a two and a half inch square, using the ruler and pencil. Cut the square into two triangles. Next, cut a three and a half inch long piece of duct tape and lay it on a flat surface with the sticky side up. Center one of the triangles on the strip and fold each side up over the edge and onto the cardstock, completely covering the other side. Do this with the second triangle as well. Cut a two and a half inch long strip of duct tape and cut it in half lengthwise. Starting at the tip, tape the two triangles together all the way down one side. Do the same with the other side. This will leave the third side open.

That's all there is to it. To use your bookmark, simply slide it over the corner of a page to mark where you're reading.

Duct Tape Clutch

Young ladies love this cute little clutch, but you don't have to be young to make one or use it. It is very easy to make.

You will need:

- Duct tape.

- Ruler.

- Scissors.

- Velcro dots.

- Embellishments.

Make a 12-by-10-inch duct tape sheet. You can make one side plain and the other patterned or you can create it using a single color. You can sandwich poster board or fabric in between the layers of tape to strengthen the sheet, but you will have a more difficult time creating folds if you do.

Turn the sheet so that it is 10 inches tall. Measure the sheet four and a half inches from the bottom to make a crease. Fold the edge upward. Measure four and a half inches from the top and fold this down to make another crease.

Cut two four-inch-long strips of tape. Hold the bottom crease up, unfold the top crease, and keep it open. Use the tape on either side to make a seam from the bottom up; this will make the pocket for the clutch. Place it evenly on both sides of the clutch to hold it closed. Place a Velcro dot on the body of the purse and affix its mate under the flap of the upper fold to hold the clutch closed. Now that your clutch is finished, you can decorate it any way you wish.

Duct Tape Drawer Organizer

This drawer organizer can be made several ways, but this way is the easiest. You can organize pencils, rubber bands, paper clips, post it notes, or other items this way.

You will need:

- Empty cereal boxes.

- Duct tape.

- Scissors.

- Ruler.

Cut the boxes to one inch less than the height of the drawer. Cover both sides of the box piece with duct tape. Cut more until you have as many sections as you need. Tape the sections together with more tape and place the completed organizer in the drawer.

Duct Tape Frame

You can use this to frame wall hangings or for photos and other artwork. This frame involves a little more than just slapping some duct tape on a frame. The stirring sticks add a little interesting texture.

You will need:

- A cheap frame of any type with wide borders.

- Coffee stir sticks.

- Duct tape.

- Scissors.

The object is to place the sticks in bundles on the frame and tape them down. Place bundles of the sticks so they fit on the frame going all around and strap them down with tape. Rub slightly so you get the imprint of the sticks on the tape. You may have to cut the sticks so they fit on the frame and that is fine. Work on the long sides of the frame first and then proceed with the shorter sides.

Duct Tape Key Chain

This key chain is just a big loop of duct tape with a hole punched in the bottom and a key ring inserted. The tape makes it pretty rigid and easy to find.

You will need:

- Ruler.

- Duct tape.

- Scissors.

- Hole punch.

- Key ring.

Measure and cut a 12-inch strip of duct tape. Lay it sticky side up on a flat surface and carefully fold it over lengthwise with the sticky sides together. Trim any uneven edges. Bring the ends together to create a loop. Take a small piece of tape and make a seam at the bottom by sticking half on one side of the end and half on the other side. Trim as needed. Punch a hole just above that seam and insert a metal key ring.

Duct Tape Lanyard

Many workplaces want their staff to wear id at all times, so this lanyard is ideal. You can make lanyards using all sorts of colors and patterns. You can even adjust the length to suit your needs.

To make the lanyard, follow the instructions for the above key ring, but add a metal clip to the key ring that will secure your identification card.

Duct Tape Refrigerator Magnet

I arranged a group of these on my refrigerator to look like I had a patchwork quilt hanging there. They are easy enough to pull apart when I need to use them.

You will need:

- Magnetic sheets.

- Duct tape.

- Scissors.

Cut the magnetic sheets in one- or two-inch squares. Cut the duct tape into one and a half or two and a half inch squares, depending on the size of the magnets you're using.

Place a magnet in the very center of the sticky side of the duct tape, and wrap the tape over the edges. You can use a permanent marker to write numbers or letters of the alphabet for young children, if you want.

Duct Tape Rose Pens

Rose Pen Made From Duct Tape

You use barrel pens for this project; the rose sets on top with the pen as its stem.

You will need:

- Green duct tape.

- Any other color of duct tape for the rose.

- Barrel pen.

- Scissors.

- Ruler.

- Plastic mat.

Cut 23 two-inch-square pieces of tape for a large rose or 11 two-inch-square pieces of tape for a small rose. Lay all the pieces on the mat with sticky sides up. Fold one corner down to almost halfway across the first square, forming a triangle. Leave a half inch of the sticky side uncovered at the bottom of the square. Take the other corner of the square and fold it over to meet the first fold in the middle of the tape square. This turns the top of the tape into a triangle. The piece should look like a wide triangle with a stripe of stickiness at the bottom. Do the same with all the squares, then trim all the petals slightly rounded at the bottom, where the sticky side is showing.

Wrap the pen with a long piece of green tape, starting just above the tip and wrapping it to an inch from the top of the pen. Leave an inch or so of extra tape hanging loose for now.

Create the center of the rose by rolling one of the triangular pieces around the top of the pen with the cut/rounded side facing the top of the pen. Use the sticky side to attach it to the pen. Continue to attach triangles to the pen. Keep the rounded sides facing the top. Slightly overlap the petals. When you've attached the last petal, continue to wrap your green tape around the pen, covering and securing the bottom layer of petals.

Make the sepals of the flower by cutting two two-inch squares out of green duct tape. Make two triangles with a sticky strip at the bottom. Wrap these around the stem at the base of your rose, one on each side of the flower.

Duct Tape Tablet Cover

In this project you need a little fabric, over which the tape is placed. I like using muslin, but you can use any type of loosely woven material except for silk.

You will need:

- Ruler.

- 1/3 yard loosely woven fabric.

180

- Duct tape.

- Rolling pin.

- Plastic mat.

Cut a fabric piece 10 3/4 inches wide by 22 inches long, or what will fit your tablet with a little extra space. Cut a piece of duct tape 10 1/2 inches long. Starting at the top, attach the tape across the top edge of the fabric. Cut a similar piece of duct tape and overlap the first strip slightly. Keep on going until the fabric is completely covered with duct tape. Press a rolling pin over the piece to remove any wrinkles or air bubbles. Turn the piece over and do the same on the side where the fabric is showing.

Cut a piece of tape that is longer than one edge. Stick half of the width on one edge and wrap it over to the other side to form a clean border. Do this for all four edges. You now have a large rectangle with borders all around.

Set your tablet on top of the sheet and fold the sheet over, extending it one to one and a half inches beyond the top of the tablet. Pinch the bottom fold to make a crease. Use the sheet that extends beyond the top of your tablet to form a flap. Tape the seams together with strips of duct tape.

Cut a 22-inch piece of tape. This will be turned into a strap to keep the flaps closed. Fold the piece in half lengthwise with sticky sides together. Wrap the strip loosely around the tablet cover and tape it down near the end of the strap.

Duct Tape Tote Bag

This tote bag is made by creating sheets of duct tape. You do this by laying several overlapping pieces down, sticky side up, and applying additional strips – sticky side down – to match them. You can use a different color of tape for the inside if you prefer. You can also make a stiffer tote by sandwiching poster board or muslin between the duct tape layers.

You will need:

- Duct tape.

- Ruler.

- Scissors.

- Fabric or poster board – optional.

This bag is made in several sections that are later taped together. Here are the tape sheets you will need to make:

- 2 sheets, nine-by-seven inches for the sides.

- 1 sheet, four by nine inches for the bottom.

- 2 sheets, four by seven inches for the width of the bag.

- 20-inch-long strip for the carrying strap.

Create the sheets above, trimming to size as necessary. Tape the sides to the bottom and then connect the sides to each other. Do this by placing the right sides together and sticking a strip of tape so that it is situated near the edge and goes over to the edge of the other piece. Flip up and do the same on the outside edge. Once the bag is taped together, use a few small pieces of tape to attach the strap to the narrow sides of the bag on the inside and; reinforce the handle by adding several strips of tape along the handle before it reaches the top of the bag. Use half-width strips of duct tape to finish the top edge of the tote

Duct Tape Wall Hangings

These wall hangings look professional and no one will ever guess you made them. I enjoy painting abstracts, but you can just as easily make flowers or animals and stick them on.

You will need:

- Canvas (either flat or framed).

- Duct tape – sheets work better but you can use roll tape too.

- Scissors.

- Pencil.

- Paper.

Draw on paper the picture you want to put on the canvas, then cut out large shapes to use as templates. Cover the canvas with background tape. If you are creating a landscape, start at the top of the canvas with white, then light blue, darker blue all the way down to the grass and green tape. Use the paper templates to cut the tape out and stick it on the canvas where it needs to go. Layer it on as you wish.

Duct Tape Wallet

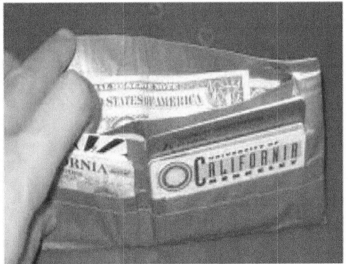

Wallet Made From Duct Tape

This project is what started the duct tape craze. These wallets are pretty durable and you can make them out of a range of printed and colored duct tape varieties.

You will need:

- Duct tape.

- Scissors.

- Plastic mat (flat plastic cutting sheet).

- Ruler.

- Credit card (for measurement only).

Cut four ten-inch-long pieces of tape and lay them on a plastic mat with the sticky sides up. Move the strips side by side lengthwise, overlapping the edges slightly. Cut another 10-inch strip and lay it, sticky side down, across the bottom strip. Do the same with three other strips. You now have a solid sheet of duct tape with no sticky sides.

Fold the sheet in half to form a wallet shape. Cut an 18-inch piece of tape and lay it, sticky side up, on the mat. Cut another sheet in half and place it, sticky side down, atop the first strip. Cut one more 18-inch piece and tear it in half, lengthwise. Set this aside for now; it will be used to enclose the top edge.

To make credit card pockets you'll need a credit card to measure against. Cut four strips of tape a quarter-inch longer on all sides than the credit card. Cut another piece of tape longer than the length of the wallet. Tear it in half lengthwise and finish the edges of the short sides of the wallet by sticking the tape close to the edge, flipping the wallet over, and wrapping the tape over to the other side.

Fold the wallet in half and place the four credit card pockets inside it. Cut a four-inch piece of tape and tear it in half lengthwise. Press this up the center, covering the pockets on one side to hold them in. Fold the end over but don't tape shut the pocket for the paper money. Instead, tuck the end inside the wallet. Use four-inch pieces to cover the outer edges of the pockets and fold them over to secure the edges. Place another strip of half-width tape along the bottom to finish that edge.

SUGGESTION: Make the back of the wallet a little higher than the front and cover all the edges with tape.

Washi Tape Binder Clips

These binder clips will bring a smile to the lips of anyone who works in an office. Make them out of the large or medium-sized binder clips. When you use the itty-bitty binder clips, the project can be a challenge, but still, it's not impossible.

You will need:

- Binder clips.

- Scissors.

- Washi tape.

Cut washi tape to fit on the binder clip and stick it on. That is all there is to it.

Washi Tape Coasters

You want these coasters to be waterproof, so the washi tape will be permanent on this project.

You will need:

- Tiles or cardboard.

- Felt tabs if using tile.

- Washi tape.

- Mod Podge.

- Foam brush.

If using cardboard, cut it into three inch squares. Cover the top of the tile completely with washi tape, layering strips so that they overlap slightly. Do the same with the cardboard, but cover both sides. Spread Mod Podge on the front of each coaster. Let the Mod Podge dry completely before adding a second coat.

If you are making the coasters from cardboard, you are finished. With the tile coaster, you'll want to put felt tabs in each corner to prevent the tile from scratching your furniture. You can hot-glue a square of felt the same size as the tile to the bottom, if you prefer.

Washi Tape Chopsticks

We eat with chopsticks at our house frequently. I have tons them and this is a way to personalize them. The only problem is that you can't immerse the whole chopstick in water to wash it, or the tape will fall off. You can keep the upper part of the stick out of the water and wash the part that comes in contact with the mouth, however.

You will need:

- Wooden chopsticks.

- Washi tape.

- Scissors.

Wrap the upper half of the chopstick in washi tape.

Washi Tape Flower Pot

You can put the washi tape on and let it go, but the likelihood of it getting wet is high when a plant is in the pot. To make your washi tape more durable, a cover of Mod Podge will make it water-resistant. Just remember that once the tape is covered with Mod Podge you won't be able to remove it.

You will need:

- A terra cotta or plastic flower pot.

- Matching saucer (optional).

- Washi tape.

- Ruler.

- Scissors.

- Mod Podge.

- Plastic disposable plate.

- Foam brush.

Cut a strip of washi tape long enough to fit around the flat rim of the flower pot. Stick it to the flat rim at the top of the pot. If you're using a saucer as well, place another strip around the rim of the saucer. Pour some Mod Podge onto the plate and use the foam brush to cover the washi tape strips. Let everything dry completely before using the pot.

Washi Tape Gift Tags

These are great for the holidays or for birthdays.

You will need:

- Card stock.

- Scissors.

- Hole punch.

- Ribbon.

- Washi tape.

Cut cardstock as large as you would like in a rectangle or a square. Cover both sides with washi tape. Punch a hole near one edge and insert a length of ribbon tied in a loop.

Washi Tape Monogram Wall Hanging

This is the perfect gift for a baby shower when the parents know beforehand the name of the baby to be born.

You will need:

- Flat canvas.

- Wooden initials.

- Acrylic paint.

- Brush or foam brush.

- Washi tape.

- Hot glue and glue gun.

Paint the canvas background color and let it dry. Paint the wood initials, if you desire, and wait for them to dry before you proceed.

Apply washi tape. You can apply it in parallel stripes or wrap it around the letters in a big spiral; use your imagination. Glue the letters (initials) onto the canvas and it will be ready to hang.

Washi Tape Notebook

Transform an old spiral notebook into a work of art with washi tape.

You will need:

- Spiral notebook.

- Washi tape.

- Scissors.

There are several ways you can decorate a notebook cover with washi tape. You can use the tape to make stripes, plaid, rays, dots, words or initials. I have one notebook in my kitchen that says "RECIPES" across it in washi tape with cupcakes printed on it.

Washi Tape Pens

Kids love these because they can personalize their own writing instruments. A friend of mine takes them to her office to keep them from wandering off into other hands. I'm sure you'll find plenty of uses for these.

You will need:

- Stick pens.

- Washi tape.

- Scissors.

Cut a strip of washi tape the same length as the barrel of the pen and roll it lengthwise into the strip. It should cover completely with just a little overlap at the seam. Smooth the tape carefully to release any air bubbles.

Washi Tape Phone Cover

Use an old phone cover to make something new and when you get tired of what you have, remove all the tape and start over with some different tape.

You will need:

- Old phone cover.

- Washi tape.

- Scissors.

- Craft knife.

Wash down the phone cover with alcohol using cotton balls. Let it dry completely. Cut washi tape and cover surface completely with slightly overlapping tape strips. Wrap the tape over to the back side when you reach the edges. Cut out areas for the camera and the flash. Snap the cover back on your phone and you're good to go.

Washi Tape Photo Frames

The results of this project look simply beautiful. You'd never know by looking at it how easy this one is to make. It takes very little time and is quite inexpensive.

This is a simple solution for last minute gift giving. It consists of covering a cheap frame with washi tape, inserting a photo, and presto, you have a delightful gift!

You will need:

- Inexpensive small frame.

- Photo.

- Washi tape.

- Scissors.

Remove the glass from the frame. Cut strips of washi tape the same length as the sides, then apply them to the frame. Complete the two long sides first before tackling the short ones. Insert a photo and replace the glass.

Washi Tape Sunglasses

Make an old pair of cheap sunglasses into a spectacular item using washi tape.

You will need:

- Cheap sunglasses.

- Washi tape.

- Scissors.

Wrap the earpieces of the sunglasses with washi tape. The tape can be easily replaced when you want to change your color scheme or style.

Washi Tape Switchplate

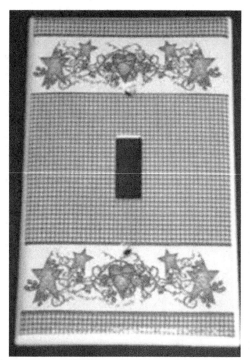

Enhance your light switches with washi tape.

Use a new plastic switchplate for this project and cover it with washi tape for décor on the wall.

You will need:

- Plastic switchplate.

- Rubbing alcohol.

- Cotton balls.

- Washi tape.

- Scissors.

- Craft knife.

- Ice pick.

Wash down the switchplate with alcohol using cotton balls. Let it dry completely. Cut washi tape and cover the switch plate completely with slightly overlapping tape strips. Wrap the tape over to the back side when you reach the edges. Cut an "X" where the switch goes, fold the cut tape over to the back of the switchplate, and stick it firmly. Poke open the screw holes with an ice pick or another sharp object. Reinstall the switchplate and you're good to go.

Washi Tape Vase

I love washi tape because it doesn't have to stay the same. If you want to change things up, you can always remove the tape and replace it with another color or pattern.

You will need:

- A glass or plastic vase.

- Washi tape.

- Scissors.

Place a strip of washi tape around the middle of the vase, around the rim, and/or around the bottom. The tape will add a touch of class to an otherwise boring object.

Chapter 9: Button Crafts

Shank Buttons (Leather at top)

Buttons come in all shapes, colors, and sizes; they can range from stark simplicity to the highly elaborate. You can find novelty buttons shaped like ducks, kittens, ice cream cones, etc. There are also regular buttons that span the hues of the rainbow. For these craft projects, you will use either a flat button or a shank button. Flat buttons have either two or four holes punched straight through the button; this allows them to be sewn onto fabric. Shank buttons have a loop behind the button, through which thread is passed to fasten the button to its fabric.

Button projects are fun to make. They make great gifts for family and friends. Who knows? You might even be able to sell a few. You can find buttons in large grab bags at craft stores or you can purchase them individually. The more intricate buttons will be a little pricier, but regular buttons can be purchased quite inexpensively.

Button Greeting Cards

Buttons On Greeting Card

The possibilities are endless when you combine buttons with greeting cards. The buttons can become the wheels of a bike, they can serve as balloons, become heads, or appear as the center of a daisy. You can turn buttons into apples on a tree or leaves in autumn.

You will need:

- Scissors.

- Ruler.

- Card stock.

- Buttons.

- Hot glue and glue gun.

- Markers or acrylic paint and paintbrush.

Cut cardstock to the desired size or purchase blank greeting cards. You must use heavy card stock because buttons are heavy and regular paper will not support them. Print or freehand draw a design on the front of the card with a sentiment inside. Glue the buttons on to complete the design.

Autumn Tree Wall Hanging

I love this wall hanging. It is very easy to make. You will create a graduated blue to green background, fronted by a tree trunk and its branches.

You will need:

- Raised canvas.

- Acrylic paint and brush or foam brush.

- Bright autumn-colored buttons in various sizes.

- Hot glue and glue gun.

Flat buttons work best for this project, although you can use shank buttons, if you first cut off their shanks. Paint the top two thirds of the canvas blue, starting with dark blue at the top and lightening the shade as you move downwards. Paint the grass, starting with dark green at the bottom of the canvas and lightening the shade as you work upward to meet the light blue in the center. Let the canvas dry thoroughly.

Next, you will paint in a tree trunk and add clearly defined branches. Let the paint dry before you proceed. Finally, you will glue the buttons onto the branches to serve as leaves. Since it is autumn, you will want to glue some "fallen leaves" – in the form of buttons – onto the grass as well.

Button Bookmark

You will need a large shank button for this project to prevent it from being swallowed up in the pages of your book. I used a one-inch diameter button and it worked fine.

You will need:

Large plastic-covered, colored paper clips

- Shank button.

- Hot glue and glue gun.

- Felt.

- Scissors.

Thread the shank button onto a paperclip until it reaches the top, the single bend.
Squeeze a little hot glue on the shank to secure the button to the paper clip. Cut out a circle of felt that is just a little smaller than the button and hot glue it to the back of the button, over the paper clip. This will doubly secure it. To use this bookmark, you will clip it to the top of the page you are reading.

Button Bowl

You can make a unique bowl using buttons. The balloon will provide the supporting structure; you will glue the buttons over it.

You will need:

- Flat buttons.

- Round inflatable balloon.

- Paper or plastic cup.

- School glue.

- Paintbrush or foam brush.

- Mod Podge.

- Scissors.

I suggest you fasten the knotted end of your balloon to your work surface before you begin. This will make it much easier to work with.

Use the brush to spread glue over the bottom half of the balloon. Allow this to partially dry before you start adding a second coat of glue in sections, sticking buttons on as you go. Set the buttons closely together, with their sides touching. When you have completely covered the glued surface, turn the balloon stem-side up, setting your button bowl on the cup to dry. Let it set for five to six hours.

Spread Mod Podge over the buttons and let your bowl dry overnight. Add another layer of Mod Podge and let it dry thoroughly.

After everything is completely dry, you can pop the balloon and carefully peel it off the bowl. It will look like you magically caused a bunch of buttons to make a bowl shape. This bowl is not water resistant, but it will make a great centerpiece for a table or an accent piece for any display.

Button Bracelet

Buttons make very cute bracelets. For this project you cannot use shank buttons. Only use buttons that have four holes and are somewhat flat.

You will need:

- Suede string.

- Large, four-hole, flat buttons.

Measure enough string to go around the wrist with 12 inches in excess. Thread the string through two holes of the button so that the ends of the string come out on the backside of the button. Do not pull it tight, but leave a loop in front of the button. Push one end of the string, from back to the front, through an unused hole in the button and pull the string through to the front. Do the same with the other string end, passing it through the last free hole in the button. You should now have one loop at the front of the button with two string ends sticking out.

Pull the string ends up until the string is tight. Now you have two ends and no loose loop. Take the ends and tie them to the string at the end in a loop big enough to hold the button down. Wrap the string around your wrist and catch the button in the loop. It should be tight around the wrist, but not too tight. If it is too loose, you may need to cut the ends a little shorter and tie it in a loop to hold the button snugly.

Button Calendar

This calendar is perfect for the person who does a lot of sewing. It is also a cute addition to any kitchen. You can use different colors of buttons to mark special days if you want. You can use all the same color buttons for every day or you can specify certain colors for certain days of the week or certain weeks in the month. With all the variety possible, you can do almost anything you can imagine.

You will need:

- 31 flat buttons, all the same size.

- Cardstock.

- Scissors.

- Marker.

- Glue.

- Flat tacks.

- Bulletin board covered in fabric of your choice.

- Felt rectangle for month date.

- Fabric paint.

- Velcro dots.

Cut the cardstock to fit inside the rim of each button. Write numbers one to 31 with marker on the cardstock circles and glue them to the front of the buttons. Glue a tack head to the back of each button. Cut 12 rectangles of felt and write the 12 months on them. Place a couple Velcro dots on the bulletin board, where the months will be placed. Attach their mates to the backs of the twelve months, matching the location.

Line up the tack buttons to make the calendar and change them out every month. I made some blank button tacks to use in months that did not have 31 days and for February, to fill out its 28 or 29 days.

Button Cars

- These are great fun for kids and make them with different color buttons for races.

- **You will need:**

- Alligator-style wooden clothespins.

- Drinking straws.

- Twist ties.

- Scissors.

- Wooden skewer.

- 1-inch diameter flat, four-hole buttons for wheels.

- Small buttons.

- Acrylic paint and brush (optional).

- Tacky glue.

Paint the clothespins if you wish, and let them dry. Thread a twist tie through one of the wheel buttons so the middle of the tie holds the button through a loop. Cut the straw so it is a bit longer than the short width of the clothespin. Thread the twist tie through the straw and into the holes of another wheel button. Place it on the bottom of the clothespin and twist it to secure by rotating the buttons. They should still be able to move but be tight against the clothespin. Do the same with the other wheel buttons and attach to the other end of the clothespin.

On the clip-side of the clothespin, there will be a hole when the clothespin is not open. Put tacky glue in that hole and clip it over the straw of the first set of wheels you made. Insert a small button between the jaws of the clothespin so it shows out front and the straw is not squished between the jaws. Place some glue between the pinchers of the clothespin right near the end. Insert the other straw with button wheels and let the glue dry.

Button Clock

This clock is easy to make and looks cute in any sewing or craft room. It also is a nice addition to the kitchen. You can use the same buttons across the board or vary the size, shape, and color

You will need:

- Burlap.

- Embroidery hoop.

- Embroidery thread.

- Buttons.

- Needle and thread or hot glue and glue gun.

- Battery powered clock hands assembly.

- Scissors or craft knife.

Cut the burlap to about four inches larger than the embroidery hoop. Center it in the embroidery hoop and clamp it down. I used embroidery floss to stitch from the edge, over the hoop to the back making a whipstitch to secure the fabric on the hoop by stitching over the hoop. You will need this added support because the clock assembly is heavy and can pull the burlap out of the hoop. If you are using a lightweight burlap, use two layers of the fabric. Cut the edges of the burlap close to the hoop.

Sew or glue the buttons following the position of the numbers of the clock. Insert the clock assembly into the center of the burlap in the embroidery hoop, per the manufacturer's instructions and hot glue the clock assembly to the back of the burlap and its hoop. Insert a battery and your clock will be ready to hang on the wall.

Button-Encrusted Vase

You can cover a vase entirely or opt for a stripe around the middle... or you can try a random placement of buttons. Do whatever catches your fancy.

You will need:

- Buttons (flat buttons work best for this project).

- Glass vase.

- Glue gun and glue.

That's about all the instructions you'll need. Now, go on and have some fun!

Button Keychain

This keychain is cute besides being easy to find in your pocket or purse.

You will need:

- Key ring with an attached chain.

- 7-millimeter jump rings.

- Small buttons (the jump ring must close when threaded through a hole in the button).

- Needle nose pliers.

Thread a jump ring through one of the holes in the button by twisting it open with the pliers. Thread an end through one of the chain links and press it closed. Do this with multiple buttons up and down the length of the chain.

Button Lampshade

Use buttons and hot glue to make a delightful lampshade.

You will need:

- Lampshade.

- Hot glue and glue gun.

- Buttons.

Flat buttons are more suited for this project because you want them to lay flat on the lampshade. However, if you remove the shank, you can use shank buttons just as easily. Usually, wire cutters are sufficient to do the job.

Glue the buttons onto the lampshade in any design you can imagine. This is one place where random placement can be highly effective.

Button Magnet

These magnets look cute on the refrigerator or on a file cabinet at work.

You will need:

- Big flat buttons with four holes.

- Smaller flat buttons that will fit inside the big ones.

- Magnetic sheet.

- Glue and glue gun.

Glue the little button on top of the big one, centering it. Cut a circle out of the magnetic sheet that is just a little smaller than the large button. Glue this to the back of the button. When the glue is set, your buttons are ready to stick to anything that is metal.

Button Magnets With Clothespin Holders

These magnets clip papers together using alligator-type clothespins covered with buttons.

You will need:

- Wooden alligator-type clothespins.

- Acrylic paint.

- Paintbrush or foam brush.

- Buttons.

- Adhesive magnet sheet.

- Glue and glue gun.

Paint your wooden clothespins and let them dry. Glue buttons to the front side of the clothespin. Cut a strip from the magnetic sheet that will fit against the backside of the clothespin, then stick it there. When everything is dry, you can slap it on your refrigerator and use it to clip papers or hold pictures in place.

Button Napkin Rings

This napkin holder is made by sewing buttons onto elastic. You will find it a classy addition to your next formal dinner.

You will need:

- Flat buttons.

- Wide elastic.

- Scissors.

- Needle .

- Thread.

Cut a strip of wide elastic to fit snugly around a napkin, about two inches long. Sew buttons onto the elastic; you want them to overlap and leave no empty space, except for a quarter inch at each end. Fold the ends of the elastic together with the buttons inside. Use the needle and thread to whip stitch the elastic together. Turn the elastic right side out and it will be ready to grace your table, holding your fanciest napkin.

Button Pencil Holders

This unique organizer will hold all your pencils and pens for ready use. The buttons can add a touch of whimsy to your desk.

You will need:

- Empty soup can.

- Poster board, white or complementary to the color of the buttons.

- Ruler.

- Scissors.

- Glue and glue gun.

- Buttons.

Use a can with only one end removed. Measure the space between the top and bottom rims and cut a strip of poster board that will fit the height and will wrap completely around the can, with a slight overlap. Glue the poster board to the can, giving you a flat surface on which to work. Use colored poster board or paint it to provide a complementary or contrasting background for your button art. Glue the buttons to the can with hot glue in any configuration you like.

Button Picture Frame

Buttons can spruce up a plain picture frame, adding whimsy or elegance. Frames make great gifts and this one in particular will definitely be something unique.

You will need:

- Inexpensive wooden or metal frame with borders wide enough to hold buttons.

- Buttons.

- Hot glue and glue gun.

Remove the glass from the frame before starting. This is an easy craft, just be careful not to burn your fingers; the glue will come up through the buttonholes and can burn you if you are not careful.

Start gluing buttons around the frame. I begin with smaller ones covering the face of the frame almost completely. I then start layering, leaving the really pretty and unusual buttons for the top layer. When you are done, fill in any small gaps with tiny buttons or beads. When all the glue has cooled, put a photo in the frame and replace the glass.

Button Pillows

The possible variations on these accent pillows are unending. In this project, you either use an existing pillow or make a pillowcase from two pieces of fabric. In either case, you'll sew buttons on your pillow in any configuration you desire.

You will need:

- Pencil or chalk marker.

- Buttons.

- Needle and thread.

- Pillowcase for an accent pillow or an existing pillow.

If you're using an existing pillow, you'll want to deconstruct it first, removing the pillow form or stuffing and then undoing at least a couple of the seams. On the pillow's face, sketch the design you want your buttons to follow. Your design can be as elaborate or as stark as you wish. Sew on your buttons in an orderly manner, following your sketch marks. If you want, you can use contrasting colors of buttons to fill in between the lines.

Once the buttons are in place and are looking the way you want them, sew the pillow together, and fill it with a pillow form or some stuffing.

Button Purse

Use a ready-made cloth tote bag or clutch for this project. If you can sew the buttons on, use quilting thread because of its durability. If it's impossible to sew them on, just use hot glue and a glue gun. You can ornament a small area, you can embellish the purse with stripes, or you can cover the whole thing with buttons.

You will need:

- Cloth tote or clutch.

- Buttons.

- Quilting thread and needle or hot glue and glue gun.

- Pencil (optional).

Sketch your design on the fabric with a pencil and then start sewing or gluing on the buttons. It usually works best to start with the larger buttons and then use smaller buttons to fill in the gaps.

Button-Rimmed Flowerpot

The upper rim of a terra cotta flowerpot is just the right surface for buttons. There are several different ways to make a button flowerpot. The first is to position them all around the rim. Another method is to create geometric designs on the side of the flower pot. Spirals are nice. You can also make little flowers, using a small button in the center and five larger buttons surrounding it and overlapping to form the petals

You will need:

- A flowerpot.

- Buttons.

- Hot glue and glue gun.

All you need to do is glue the buttons on the flowerpot. If you wish, you can paint the flowerpot with acrylic paint before gluing on the buttons.

Button Thumbtacks

These thumbtacks will lend some pizzazz to your bulletin board.

You will need:

- Thumbtacks (not pushpins).

- Piece of scrap wood or foam core.

- Glue and glue gun.

- Shank buttons or flat buttons.

- Metal clippers or sharp wire cutters.

To make it easy to glue onto the top of the thumbtacks, you'll want to press your thumbtacks partway into a piece of wood or foam core. If you have shank buttons, you'll want to remove the shank on the back by clipping it off using wire cutters. With flat buttons, you can glue together a stack of several of them. When the glue is set, then you can glue your stack of buttons onto the head of the tack.

Button Welcome Wreath

I have made these using red and green buttons for Christmas, also white and blue for a friend during Hanukkah. However, you can use your favorite color combinations. I like to combine dark forest green, cranberry, and a beige color. A mixture of blues and greens can present an intriguing wreath against a white door. For Halloween you can use yellow, white, and orange to mimic candy corn. Of course, there's always red and pink with a little white thrown in for Valentine's Day.

You will need:

- Cardboard (optional: Styrofoam ring).

- Scissors or craft knife.

- Acrylic paint and brush or foam brush.

- Buttons .

- Ribbon.

- Hot glue and glue gun.

Cut a piece of cardboard into the shape of a wreath. Do not make it too large or the buttons will make it quite heavy. The perfect size is around 10 inches in diameter, but you can make it smaller if you like.

Paint the cardboard a base color that will complement the color of your buttons. Start with smaller buttons, flat and unattractive ones that can fill in the space. Layer some more interesting buttons on top and reserve the top layer for the really striking and unusual ones. You can use shank buttons by cutting off the shank. Fill in any gaps as best you can with small buttons or beads and let everything dry. Tie a large strip of ribbon around the wreath in a loop so you can hang it on your door.

Button Wreath On Canvas

This project is similar to the button welcome wreath, but in this case you create it on canvas. These instructions describe creating a white button wreath over a blue background, but you can use any colors you like.

You will need:

- Raised canvas.

- Royal blue acrylic paint.

- Paintbrush or foam brush.

- Pencil and a piece of string.

- White buttons of different sizes.

- Small white beads of various sizes.

- Ribbon bow.

Paint the canvas a solid royal blue and let it dry. Make a compass out of a pencil tied to a string. Hold the string in the center of the canvas and use the pencil to draw a large circle a couple inches inside the borders of the canvas. Draw a smaller circle to define the inner border of the wreath. Your wreath can be as narrow or as wide as you wish.

Starting on the outer edge of the wreath, glue buttons around it, keeping the edge as even as possible. Keep adding buttons side by side, working inward until you have reached the inner boundary of the wreath. Now start overlapping and layering buttons to fill in the wreath completely. You'll want to vary the size and pattern of your buttons to create interesting texture. Fill in any remaining gaps with small buttons, using small beads for the tiniest spots.

When you can't find any more empty spaces to set buttons or beads, you're finished. Now you can make a bow using the ribbon and glue it to the top or bottom of the wreath, whatever looks best to you. Hang your finished work on the wall as is or set the canvas in an open frame, with no glass to cover it.

Button Monogram

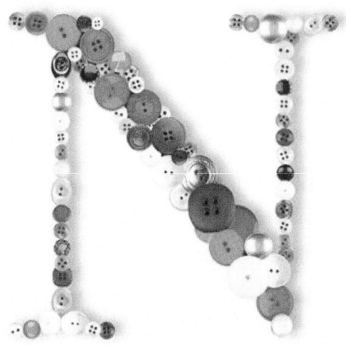

Button initials add color and texture to a room.

These button initials are great for a kid's room; they can also add a touch of whimsy to a guest room.

You will need:

- Wooden letters that hang on the wall.

- Acrylic paint and brush.

- Hot glue and glue gun.

- Buttons.

Paint your letters a solid background color and let them dry completely before proceeding. Glue buttons onto the letters, starting with larger buttons and filling in with smaller ones. When the front sides of the letters are completely covered with buttons, let them dry, then you'll be free to hang them up wherever you'd like.

Cute-As-A-Button Hair Clip

Use a metal hair clip that closes and opens when you bend it. They kind of have an elongated heart shape to them.

You will need:

- Buttons.

- Hot glue and glue gun.

- Hair clips.

Open the hair clip and glue the button onto the front head of the clip. Let it dry overnight before using.

Embroidered Napkins With Buttons

These napkins are cute and will enhance any teatime. They will also add class to a formal dinner and look great held by the button napkin rings described earlier in this chapter.

You will need:

- Cloth napkins.

- Embroidery thread and needle.

- Scissors.

- Embroidery hoops.

This is one case where less is more. Because the napkin is a functional item, you want to limit your button ornamentation to a corner or a simple hem edge. I worked a single corner of my napkin and sewed buttons on in the shape of a daisy, using a yellow button for the center and five smaller orange buttons for the petals. After sewing on the buttons, you can apply the embroidery hoop and embroider curling vines, leaves, or any other embellishment.

Chapter 10: Making Jewelry

Jewelry making is a lucrative craft you can do at home and sell easily. Everyone loves jewelry; I have a friend who often sells her jewelry right off her neck and wrists.

Before you start, there are a few jewelry essentials to have on hand.

You will need:

- Needle nose jewelry pliers.

- Jewelry wire cutters.

- 14- or 20-gauge wire.

- E6000 adhesive.

- Pendant bails (the clasp that holds the pendent).

- Jump rings.

- Clasps and hooks (if you are making a necklace).

- Earring wires (if you are making earrings).

Not only can you make money with your jewelry, but it is a satisfying craft. Jewelry making doesn't take a lot of time, so you can fairly quickly accessorize your outfit before you go out. In this chapter, you will learn to make pendants, bracelets, rings and other handy items.

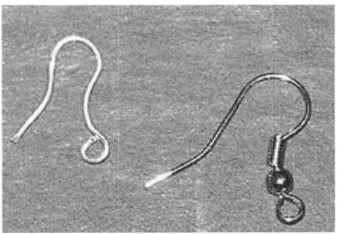

Earring Wire

Adjustable Wire Charm Bangle Bracelet

These are very popular and you can find charms just about anywhere.

You will need:

- 14-gauge wire.

- Wire cutters.

- Needle nose pliers.

- Ruler.

Cut 14 inches of wire. Bend one end upward a little less than one inch from the edge. Bend down on the other side. Close the loops around the wire but do not clamp down; it must be able to move in and out. Add charms and you are done

Woven T-Shirt Bracelet

You will need:

- Scissors.

- Ruler.

- Old T-shirts.

- Binder clip.

Remove the hem from an old T-shirt and discard it. Cut strips about one and a half inch-wide so you have circles of fabric. Cut one seam so you have one long strand. Grab both ends of the strand and pull hard. This will stop the material from curling up. You will need two 4-foot-long strips. Cut small slits that do not go through to the edge in one end of both strips. String the un-slit end of one strip through the slit in the other and then into its own slit to form a loop and pull to tighten.

Take the two strips and fold them in half. Clip at the fold with a binder clip. You now have four strands of T-shirt. Take two strands on the right and fold over two strands on the left, then loop back under and tighten.

Let's pretend we made one strip from a white T-shirt and one from a red T-shirt. We bind them together. We will take the two white strands on the right and fold over the two red strands on the left. We then loop back under the white strands and back under the red ones to make a knot and tighten.

Now take the red strands and fold over the white ones, loop back under the red and over the white and tighten. Repeat, alternating colors and tighten evenly until the knotted strand fits the wrist. Remove the clip and feed the free ends through loops and knot several times. Cut off any excess.

Ball Chain Ring

Ball chain with connector

It is hard to believe that this ring is so simple to make, yet teens just love them. You will need a necklace chain that is made of interlocked little silver balls. These chains have little oval shaped connectors that will bring the chain together in a loop.

You will need:

- Ball chain.

- Mandrel.

- Wire cutter.

- Ball chain connector.

Measure the chain on the mandrel and cut it half size larger than you normally use. If you wear a size eight ring, cut it to fit an eight and a half size.

Put a connector on one end and connect it to the other end. That is all there is to it. Now make several and stack them on your finger.

Button Pendant

Some buttons are absolutely gorgeous, so why not make pendants out of them? You'll want flat buttons for this project. While I suggest 24-gauge wire, you can get away with a lighter gauge if necessary. You also need a jewelry bail that you can find in the jewelry findings aisle in a craft store. These look like little spades with a loop; the necklace chain will go through them to suspend the pendant.

You will need:

- Buttons (one that fits on top of the other.

- 24-gauge jewelry wire.

- Jewelry bail.

- E6000 glue.

- Wire cutters.

Set the small button on top of the larger one, lining up the holes. Thread the ends of a small piece of wire through separate holes in both buttons from front to back, so that the middle of the wire shows as a loop in front. Turn the buttons over and twist the wire to tighten and hold both together. Tuck the ends of the wire into a hole to secure it. Glue the bail to the top of the button using E6000 glue and let it dry. Run a chain through the bail and you're now ready to wear your pendant.

Charm Ring

This is another really simple ring that you can put a charm on or leave it off and stack many of them on the same finger.

You will need:

- Necklace chain with open links.

- Mandrel.

- Charms .

- Small jump rings.

- Wire cutters.

- Needle nose pliers.

Cut the chain so it fits around the mandrel a half size larger than what you are making. Use the needle-nose pliers to open one of the end chain links and insert it in to the other end link so it becomes one continuous circle.

Attach a jump ring to a charm with a hole in it to accommodate the jump ring and attach it to one of the links in the chain. You can add one or more charms, according to your preference.

Crocheted Bracelet

These bracelets look really cute and they don't take much to make.

You will need:

- 1/4-inch to 1/8-inch wide ribbon.

- Gel band bracelet.

- A size J or I crochet hook.

- Scissors.

- Medium beads (optional).

Tie the ribbon onto the gel bracelet, leaving about two to three inches free. Place a crochet hook through the gel bracelet, catch the ribbon, and make a single crochet stitch. Keep crocheting simple stitches around the bracelet until the ribbon completely encases the gel band. When you reach the end, knot the ribbon again and cut it off, leaving about three inches of ribbon free at the end. Tie the free ends together into a knot and then make a small bow. You can also thread beads on each ribbon end and tie knots at their ends so the beads won't fall off.

Headpin Earring

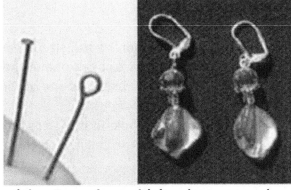

L: headpins, R: earrings with beads strung on headpins

Headpins are easily located in the "findings" section of the jewelry department of a craft store. They are long metal pins with a little loop or end piece at the bottom. They are perfect for stringing on beads and they will stay on because of that end piece.

You will need:

- 4 headpins.

- Earring wire.

- 4 four-millimeter beads.

- 8 seed beads.

- Flat nose or needle-nose pliers.

- Round nose pliers.

Note: This makes two earrings.

Thread one of the seed beads on the head pin and bring it down to the end where it will stop because of a loop or end piece. Thread one four-millimeter sized bead and one more seed bead on the headpin and bring them all the way to the end. Use the flat nose pliers to bend the head pin 90 degrees about a half inch from the open end of the headpin. Grab the very top of the open end of the headpin with needle-nose pliers and make an open-ended loop. Slide the loop through the earring wire and, using the pliers, close the loop so that the headpin cannot come off.

Make a second beaded headpin and hang it from the same earring wire, so that you have two beaded headpins hanging from one earring wire. Make the other earring, following these same instructions.

NOTE: You can string as many – or as few – beads on the headpins as you like.

Hoop Earring

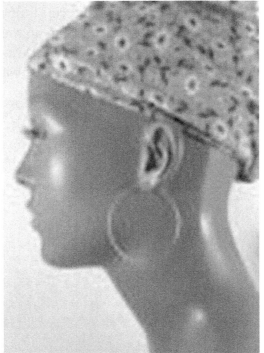

The Clean Look Of Hoop Earrings

Make your own hoop earrings with some wire and an earring wire. These hoops are about two inches in diameter, but you can make them smaller or larger as you wish. To make them perfectly round, use a round item, like a small bottle or cup as a form to bend the wire around.

You will need:

- 20- to 22-gauge wire.

- Beads (optional).

- Wire cutters and needle-nose pliers.

- Jump rings.

- Earring wires.

Cut two pieces of wire about two and a half inches long. Place these around a round object and bend them to form a circle. Slide any beads you want to use on the earrings. Take one loose end and curl it upward with pliers to create a small loop. Take the other loose end and do the same, making the loop the same size. Cross the loops so they both insert into the earring wire. Tighten the earring wire by squeezing it a little with the needle-nose pliers.

Beaded Hoop Earrings

Leather Bead Ring

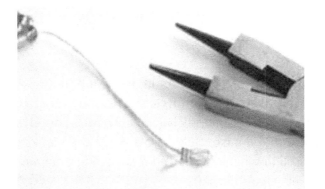

Crimp Bead Securing String Loop

This is a nice ring to wear with jeans or a leather jacket.

You will need:

- Leather string.

- Crimp beads.

- Crimp pliers or flat nose pliers.

- Small beads.

- Mandrel.

- Scissors.

Measure the leather string on the mandrel to a half size larger than the finished product. String on one crimp bead and thread on one or more additional beads, bringing them to the middle of the strand. String on another crimp bead and center everything on the leather string. Use the crimp pliers or flat nose pliers to crimp the beads so the other beads stay put.

Place one end of the leather string in the crimp bead one way and the other end going in the other way. Check the size; if the ring is too large, pull some of the leather out through the other side of the crimp bead. Use the crimp pliers or needle-nose pliers to crimp it down. Cut off any excess leather

Nail Polish Pendant

You can make these pretty pendants in any color simply by using any type of nail polish. This project calls for clear cabochons that can be purchased at any craft store. The cabochons will usually be round, oval, or square and they will fit into a metal base, called a blank. These blanks will often have a hole or stem through which you can fit a jump ring or chain. The cabochons look like flattened, clear marbles.

You will need:

- Clear cabochons and matching blanks.

- E6000 glue.

- Nail polish.

- Clear top coat polish.

Turn the cabochon over and paint the back with nail polish. Glide it on as if you are painting your nails. If you're using glittery nail polish, dab it on. Let the polish dry completely, then add another coat. Let this dry for 24 hours.

Cover the nail polish with a clear top coat and let it dry for at least 12 more hours. Smear E6000 glue on the blank and a little on the back of the cabochon before sticking the two together, wiping any excess glue off. Let this dry for 24 hours and trim any stray glue off with a craft knife.

Paint Chip Earrings

These are made with three single paint chips you find at the hardware store in the paint section. I have made some with dark blue, medium, and light blue swatches that were very pretty and became a favorite of some friends.

You will need:

- Paint chips.

- 1/2 inch, one inch, 1-1/2-inch circle punches.

- Tacky glue.

- Something to make a hole with.

- Jump rings.

- Needle nose pliers.

- Mod Podge.

- Brush.

- Earring wires.

Cut individual circles of each size from light, medium and dark shades of the same color, or you can make them all different colors. The large circle will be partially covered by the medium circle, which will be covered partially by the small circle. Cut two large circles that will be glued to the back of each earring.

Spread a thin layer of tacky glue on the back of the small circle and stick it to the medium circle, matching top edges. Apply some glue to the back of the medium circle and stick it to the large one. It should all look like one big circle with different shades at the bottom. Repeat this process to make the other earring. Use the tacky glue to stick the one large circle to the back of the circles. Paint the front of the earring with Mod Podge and let it dry, then do the same with the back.

Poke a hole in the very top of the earring near the edge and insert a jump ring, bending it so the earring cannot come out. Thread the jump ring onto the earring wire and your earrings are ready to wear.

Pearl Teardrop Earrings

These classic earrings are easy to make using beading wire and six- and eight-millimeter simulated pearls. The increments below are for making one earring, so double it for two.

You will need:

- Beading wire.

- Cutters.

- Ruler.

- 4 6–millimeter pearls.

- 1 8-millimeter pearl.

- Crimp beads.

- Crimping pliers.

- Needle nose pliers.

- Earring wire.

Cut five inches of beading wire. String on two six-millimeter pearls, one eight-millimeter pearl, and two more six-millimeter pearls. These will be the bottom of the teardrop. Thread both ends of the wire through a crimp bead and cross them, forming a teardrop with pearls at the bottom and a crimp bead at the top.

Thread the wire ends back through the crimp bead to form a small loop at the top of the crimp on the other side of the teardrop. Crimp the bead with crimping pliers or needle nose pliers. Trim any extra wire. Insert the top small loop into an earring wire.

Polymer Clay Swirl Pendant

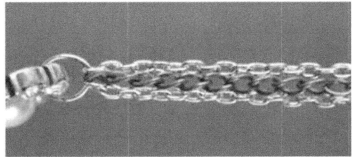

Jump Ring, Connecting Pendant (Far Left) To Chain (On Right)

Use several colors of polymer clay, making small logs, putting them side by side, and overlapping them a bit so they stick together. You can run this through a pasta maker to flatten it, twist the strands to create swirls of color, roll them into beads, or cut them into thick slices.

You will need:

- Polymer clay.

- Straw or toothpick.

- Jump rings.

- Pliers.

Make your polymer clay beads or cabochons. For beads, use a straw or toothpick to make holes all the way through them so they can be strung. If you use a slice of clay or have run it through the pasta maker and cut the clay into a shape, make a hole at the top that is large enough to accommodate a jump ring.

Bake the clay according to the package instructions. If you want it to be shiny, spray it with clear acrylic. Insert a jump ring or string the beads onto a necklace.

Popsicle Stick Bracelet

Kids and adults alike love these bracelets. They can be as simple or as intricate as you want them to be. The paint, jewels, and wood burner are suggestions for decorating the bracelet. Use whatever you prefer.

You will need:

- Pan with water on the stove.

- Jumbo Popsicle sticks.

- Drinking glass.

- Emery board.

- Acrylic paint.

- Brush.

- Stick-on jewels.

- Wood burner set.

- Mod Podge.

Boil the water in a pan and drop a few Popsicle sticks in to soak for 30 minutes. Take them out but do not dry them off. Bend the sticks around the inside of a drinking glass, at the top. Be careful, because some sticks are stubborn and can break or split, giving you a nice splinter. The dry stick should hold its curve well.

When it's dry, use an emery board to sand it smooth. You can then paint the stick with acrylic, stick on some jewels, use a wood burner to decorate it, or add just about anything you want, such as sequins, fabric, ribbon, and even scrapbook paper. Paint Mod Podge over the top and on the inside, then let everything dry completely. Apply a second coat of Mod Podge to the outside and let everything dry thoroughly before wearing.

Seashell Pendant

*If you don't have a chain, you can always use a ribbon or string
to hang this pendant around your neck.*

If you hunt your own seashells, please make sure no one alive or deceased is still in the shell when you use it for crafts. It can lead to a very smelly situation if they are. If you do not live near the seashore, most craft stores and even some dollar stores will sell you bags of shells.

A hole must be drilled in the shell in order to string it on anything. You'll want to use a dremel tool with a small bit to make the hole. You can, however purchase shells that have been pre-drilled. The best shells for this craft project are scallops or snail-type shells.

You will need:

- Shell.

- Jump rings.

- Jewelry pliers.

- Glue (optional).

- Glitter (optional).

Holes should be at the base or top of the shell. Open a jump ring and push one end through the hole. The jump ring needs to be large enough to curve above the shell and allow a chain to run through it. Close the jump ring with the pliers. Leave the shell as it is or run a line of clear glue along the edge and press in some glitter.

Soda Can Ribbon Bracelet

These shiny ribbon bracelets are fun to make...and to wear.

Who knew a soda can would make a great bracelet? Surprisingly, it molds to the wrist very nicely.

You will need:

- 1 soda can.

- Marker.

- Ruler.

- Metal cutter.

- Ribbon.

- Mod Podge.

- Foam brush.

- E6000 glue.

- Alligator clothespins.

- Scissors.

- Beads (medium-sized – the ribbon will have to pass through the holes).

Measure the ribbon width. If it is one and a half inches wide, measure one and a quarter inches down from the rim of the can on the side. Measure another one and a quarter inches down and make another mark. Measure the same all around the can and then make a line with the marker. You should have two strips. Cut these strips out. Fuse the two can strips together using E6000 glue. Clamp together with alligator clothespins. Let it dry for 1hours or more.

Cut ribbon one and a half yard longer than the can strips. You will need two of these ribbon strips. Fold them in half to find the middle of the ribbon. Make a light mark to indicate the center spot. Find the middle of the can strips and mark them. Apply Mod Podge to one side of the can strips. Apply it liberally. Find the middle marks and apply the ribbon to the can so the middle marks match and the ribbon covers the can strips. You will have excess ribbon on either side of the can strip. Clip them together with alligator clothespins. Let the Mod Podge dry.

Turn the can strip over and do the same on the other side, making and matching middle marks. Clip and let it dry. Either leave the bracelet as it is or slather Mod Podge on the ribbon on both sides of the bracelet that comes in contact with the can, and then stand on the side to let it dry. This will make the ribbon very shiny.

Once it is dry, take the two lengths of ribbon on one side of the can strip and tie in a knot close to the can strip. Take a bead and thread both ribbons (front and back) through the bead and tie in another knot under the bead. Do the same on the other side. Put the bracelet on your wrist and tie the two sides with a bow.

Tassel Earrings

Tassel earrings only add to your beauty.

Tassel earrings were made popular by Oscar De La Renta and they originally cost a fortune. Now you can make your own for a fraction of the original cost. You use nylon Japanese bunka string that falls like liquid and does not tangle. You'll unravel the string to make these earrings. I prefer using two colors of string, but you can do as you like. The ingredients list below will allow you to make a pair of earrings.

You will need:

- Japanese bunka embroidery thread, about 79 feet.

- Scissors.

- Half-inch brass bead caps.

- E6000 glue.

- 5/8-inch beads to go on top of cap.

- Eye pins.

232

- Needle nose pliers.

- Wire cutters.

- Earring wires.

Cut two pieces of bunka thread three inches long and set them aside. Cut 20 strands of bunka thread eight inches long (I divide these among two colors). Lay them on a flat surface and pick them up from the middle. Slip one of the three-inch pieces around the middle and triple knot it. Cut any excess from the three-inch piece.

Thread the eye pin up through the bottom of the bead cap so the loop of the eye pin is in the cap. Squeeze E6000 glue into the cap and stuff the knotted part of the tassel in it. Hold until it is secure. Let it dry for an hour.

Thread a bead in the top of the bead cap and, with needle-nose pliers, bend the eye pin about 90 degrees to the left and wrap it clockwise around the right side of the pliers. Move the eye pin all the way around. Grip the resulting loop with pliers and wrap the excess eye pin around the bottom of the loop two times, trimming any excess wire. Attach the ear wire to the loop and trim the tassel to an appropriate length.

Washer Necklace

These necklaces get a lot of attention. You can be as creative with the washers as you like; hardware stores carry a whole array. I prefer the bold look, using large washers and placing them on a generously long string so they hang down mid-body, but you can shorten the string to your liking.

You will need:

- Washers.

- String for necklace (I prefer silk rattail).

- Scrapbook sheets.

- Pencil.

- Scissors or craft knife and cutting board.

- Tacky glue.

- Nail file.

- Paper glaze.

- Wax paper

Turn the scrapbook sheet upside down and trace the washer on the paper with a pencil. Use a craft knife on a cutting board or scissors to cut out two of these. Use tacky glue to glue the scrapbook paper rings to both sides of the washer and let it dry completely. Use a nail file to sand the edges smooth.

Set the washer on wax paper. Paper Glaze and Glossy Accents come in a squeeze bottle. Using one of these products, start at the outside edge and squeeze it all around the edge, then start filling in the circle to the inner edge. This will create a bubble-like dome over the washer. Let this dry for 24 hours, then turn it over and do the same to the other side.

Cut a 30-inch piece of string and fold it in half. Put the folded middle through the hole in the washer and bring the ends through to catch the loop. Tie in a knot. You can add beads to the string if you want to further accessorize the necklace.

Washi Tape Earrings

Use washi tape to make a fashion statement.

Anyone will love these colorful earrings. They are simple to make, so you can now create a pair for each of your outfits.

You will need:

- Mod Podge.

- Toothpicks.

- Circle punch – whatever size you want but don't make them too small.

- Washi tape.

- White card stock.

- Something with which to punch a hole: a hammer and nail or an ice pick.

- 20-gauge wire.

- Wire cutters.

- Round and flat nose pliers.

- Earring wires.

Stick washi tape to the front and back of cardstock. Overlap them to cover the card stock entirely. Cover enough cardstock that you can punch two circles out of it. One-inch circles are perfect for this project. Lay the circles on a protected surface.

Apply the Mod Podge to one side of each circle, starting at the center with the tip of the bottle and drawing it out toward the edges. This makes a dome over the circle. Let it dry for 20 minutes and pop any air bubbles that appear carefully with a toothpick. Let it dry overnight, then turn it over and Mod Podge the other side.

Punch a hole in the top of each circle. Cut two three-inch-long pieces of wire and pull this through the hole in each earring, with one side longer than the other. Make a loop with the longer side at the top of the earring and wrap the excess around the base of the loop. Trim any excess wire and insert the earring wire.

Washi Tape Popsicle Stick Bracelet

You will need:

- Pan with water on the stove.

- Jumbo Popsicle sticks.

- Drinking glass.

- Emery board.

- Acrylic paint.

- Brush.

- Mod Podge.

Boil the water in a pan and drop a few Popsicle sticks in to soak for 30 minutes. Take them out but do not dry them off. Bend the sticks around the inside of a drinking glass, toward the top. Be careful, because some sticks are stubborn and can break or split, giving you a nice splinter. The dry stick should hold its curve well.

When it's dry, use an emery board to sand it smooth. You'll use washi tape to decorate the bracelet, however you wish. Complete it with Mod Podge and let it dry for 24 hours before wearing.

Washi Tape Washer Necklace

You will need:

- Washer (the type with smaller holes works better).

- Washi tape.

- Craft knife.

- Pencil.

- Scissors.

- Glossy accents or paper glaze.

- Wax paper.

- String for necklace.

Cover one side of the washer with strips of washi tape, going up and down with a little excess over the edge to fold over to the back of the washer. Overlap the washi tape so you can't see any of the washer. Turn the washer over and, with a craft knife, cut an "X" shape in the middle where the hole is. Turn the washer right side up and push down where you just made the "X" to stick the tape to the back side of the washer.

The front side will look finished with all edges wrapped smoothly to the back, but the backside won't look very good. To fix this, put the same kind of tape on a little square of wax paper. Place the washer on the washi tape and lightly trace around both outer and inner edges with a pencil. Cut the shape out with scissors and carefully peel the washi tape off the wax paper in one piece. Affix this ring to the backside of the washer and run your fingers around the edges to smooth it.

Set the washer on wax paper. Paper glaze comes in a squeeze bottle. Start at the outside edge and squeeze it all around the edge, then start filling in the circle to the inner edge. This will create a bubble-like dome over the washer. Let this dry for 24 hours, then turn it over and do the same to the other side.

Cut a 30-inch piece of string and fold it in half. Put the folded middle through the hole in the washer and bring the ends through to catch the loop. Tie in a knot. You can add beads to the string to further accessorize the necklace.

Wired Button Ring

The Beauty Of A Wire-Wrapped Button Ring

This ring uses a two- or 4-hole button of any size. The instructions are for a 4-hole button but you can easily adapt to one with 2 holes.

You will need:

- 18-gauge wire.

- Wire cutter.

- Button with four holes.

- Needle nose pliers.

- Mandrel.

Cut two feet of the wire and insert it through two holes in the button that are across from each other. Do not cross them. Bring the button to the middle of the wire so there are equal lengths of wire on both sides and a straight line of wire shows on the top of the button through the two holes. Flatten the wire on the button.

Hold the button with the right side out against the mandrel and wrap one side one size larger than you want the ring to be, one time. If you want it to be a size eight, wrap at size nine. Wrap the other side one time.

Take the first end of the wire and wrap it one more time. Do the same with the other end. You should still have excess wire. Wrap that excess around the ring part that goes around the finger, starting closest to the button and working away from it. Do this on both sides. Flatten the wire ends with needle-nose pliers and slightly tuck them into to the wrapping so it does not scratch your finger or get caught on clothing.

Wire Shank Button Ring

These rings are made from shank buttons.

239

These button rings can be very beautiful, but they stand up from the finger a bit, which can be hard to get used to. Shank buttons are beautiful. I have seen some that are in a frosted rose shape, some with pearls in the middle and metal filigree all around and some even have colored glass stones in them. If you can find antique shank buttons, they make wonderful rings. I made a stunning ring out of jet with a piece of real ruby set in it recently, and it used to be just a button.

You will need:

- 18-gauge wire.

- Shank button.

- Wire cutters.

- Needle-nose pliers.

- Mandrel.

Cut two feet of wire. Insert one end of the wire through the shank and bring the button to the middle of the wire, then move it so that one wire is a quarter inch longer than the other. Insert the other end of the wire in through the opposite direction. Take the short wire and loop it to bring it through the shank and secure it.

Hold the shank against the mandrel one size larger than you want the ring to be and wrap one wire around the mandrel two times. Do the same with the other wire. Take the long side and bring it up around the stem, or shank, of the button and wrap around it three times. Bring it back down. You should have excess wire; wrap that around the ring and tuck the end under, flattening it down with the pliers so that nothing rough remains.

Wire-wrapped Rings

The mandrel is a must for ring-making.

Yes, you can make your own rings with just some wire and maybe a few enhancements like stones, beads, or even buttons. One thing you do need to make rings is a mandrel. A mandrel is a long conical shaped item that is used to measure ring size. Get yours in a craft store near the "findings" department. They will have measurements on them to help you determine ring sizes.

This ring is quite simple to make; it is only made of wire. You can string some seed beads on the wire after getting it situated on the mandrel and before you shape it. You can make any shape from curlicues to hearts and more.

You will need:

- Jewelry wire, 16- to 20-gauge, your choice.

- Wire cutters.

- Round nose pliers.

- Mandrel.

Cut a piece of wire three to five inches long. Using the round nose pliers, take one end and turn it up in a small loop. Go to the other end and twist a small loop down so it is opposite the other loop.

Wrap the wire around the mandrel to a slightly larger size than you normally wear. Bring the loops together in a figure eight and bend them. Instead of just loops, cut the wire a little longer and make spirals. Add beads or a small charm.

Wire-Wrapped Stone Or Sea-Glass Pendant

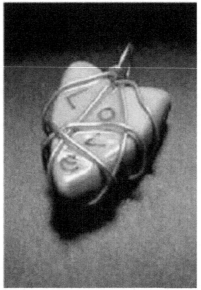

Wire-wrapped pendants are wearable modern art.

For this project you'll want to use sea glass or stones with slightly jagged edges. You don't want anything smooth, because the wire must catch on the edges to hold it in. I like to use lapis, aventurine, fluoride and other crystal or non-crystalline stones. If you use jasper or another stone that looks better wet, spray it with a clear acrylic first and let it dry before you proceed.

You will need:

- Sea glass or natural stones.

- 18-gauge wire.

- Pencil.

- Jewelry pliers and cutters.

Cut 14 inches of wire. Take the middle of the wire and curl it around a pencil two times, then twist this and remove the pencil. This is where the neck chain will run.

Rough-cut stones and sea glass can make beautiful pendants.

You now have two connected pieces of wire. Bring one straight down and bend the other one off to one side. Place the stone atop the straight wire and wrap it with the other wire several times, crossing the wires to trap the stone securely. Keep wrapping with the wire until the stone is stable, then bring the wires back up to the twisted hanger and wrap them around the base several times. Depending on the size of the stone, you may need more than 14 inches of wire.

Painted rocks (see Chapter 4) can easily be converted to wire-wrapped pendants.

Chapter 11: Yarn Crafts

Yarn crafting does not necessarily mean you have to knit or crochet, even though I have included a few simple patterns in this chapter. There are many other ways you can use yarn and other fibers to make flattering pieces for your home and office, as you will soon see.

Knitting and crochet work are for everyone.

The arts of knitting and crochet, even at this basic level, call for much more detailed instructions than I can provide in this book. Therefore, I have left knitting instruction to others and have included crochet projects that require only the most basic of stitches. With these, I have assumed you have at least a passing knowledge of how to use the basic techniques.

Crocheting can be fun and easy, once you have mastered a few basic steps. To get set up with the basics, I recommend you visit http://www.instructables.com/id/Beginning-crochet/. These animated illustrations walk you through each step, from holding the crochet hook and wrapping the yarn correctly around your opposite hand to finishing off your piece.

But enough of that; on to the projects!

Crochet-Covered Hanger

These covers can be crocheted over wire or plastic hangers.

Clothes tend to slip off plastic or wire hangers, so crochet stitching over them will prevent that from happening. Crochet-covered hangers will also prevent the creasing of your clothes. This project doesn't take much yarn, either. You can use either a plastic or a wire hanger. Crocheted hangers make great holiday gifts and are something that will be appreciated for years to come.

You will need:

- Hangers.

- Crochet hook size G (4.25 millimeters).

- Yarn needle.

- Fabric glue.

- Scissors.

Start halfway down the hook and work either right or left. Tie the yarn onto the hanger with a long tail. Drop a bit of glue on the knot to hold it in place. You can either crochet over the tail or put it through a yarn needle and weave it through at the end.

Holding the yarn on top of the hanger, start at the base of the hanger's hook, pull up a loop, and make a single crochet stitch, encasing the hanger in the loop of the stitch. Keep making single crochet stitches all around the hanger until you approach the hook. Join the first single crochet you come to on the hook, fasten it off, and weave the ends into the crochet.

You can cover this hanger with a single color of yarn or crochet two different colors together at the same time. You can also use variegated yarn to create an interesting effect.

Crochet-Enhanced Flip-flops

In this project, you will perform the same type of crochet stitch as you did with the crocheted clothes hanger a little earlier. The flip-flop bands are perfect for this. Again, use one color or two different colors at the same time.

You will need:

- Flip-flops.

- Glue.

- Size F crochet hook.

- Scissors.

- Yarn needle.

Start at one side of the flip-flop band, so you crochet down the "V" toward the toe piece and back up. Tie the yarn onto the flip-flop strap and use a little glue to secure it to the in place. Hold the yarn on top of the strap and reach under to hook the yarn, pull a loop up, and make a single crochet.

Keep going down to the toe, skip over the pin that goes down into the flip-flop and travel back up to the base of the flip-flop on the other side. When you are finished, fasten off the yarn by tying another knot and putting a little glue on the knot. Thread any tails into the yarn needle and weave them through to hide them.

Eye Of God

Eye of God , a.k.a., Ojos de Dios

A literal translation from the Spanish "ojos de Dios", these colorful wall hangings are popular in Latin American countries. They are used as good luck charms and are hung from walls, ceilings, or tree branches. They require either two sticks that are void of any leaves and twigs or two regular sized craft sticks. I love to make them from twigs because they look more natural.

You can use all sorts of wild colors when making this project. The yarn is wrapped around the twigs or sticks to form a diamond shape.

You will need:

- Twigs or craft sticks.

- Yarn in many bright colors.

- Scissors.

- Glue (superglue or hot glue).

- Tacky glue.

The twigs need to be about a quarter inch in diameter or the size thickness of a pencil, with no leaves or peeling bark. Cut them to six inches in length. Glue the two twigs or sticks into the shape of a cross and let them dry overnight.

Take one color of yarn and hold the tail with your thumb near the intersection of the cross. Put a dab of glue on the end to hold it fast to the wood. Wrap the yarn over and around the wood, making a loop around each stick before proceeding to the next one Keep on wrapping yarn around all four sticks to create a large diamond. Wrap the yarn close to the center and work outward, leaving no spaces between the strands. Go around four times with one color before you change. Glue the end of the yarn to the back of the cross. Create a hanger by tying a piece of yarn to the ends of two of the sticks. If you wish to add ornamentation, you can glue on beads, feathers, or tassels.

Pompom Bookmark

These are super easy to make and the bookmark looks like a big pompom protruding from the pages of your book. You can make them in school colors for kids.

You will need:

- Yarn.

- Scissors.

Wrap yarn around three fingers until covered in a quarter-inch layer of yarn. Cut from skein. Cut a 10-inch strand from the skein and thread under the yarn above the fingers and over the top of the yarn and tie in a knot. The knot should be in the middle with each end having a series of loops. Cut the loops free, then shake and fluff them to make the pompom. The strands from the knot should hang down. Place the strands between book pages near the binding and let the pompom stick up above the pages.

Spiral Yarn Wall Hanging

Creating A Spiral Yarn Wall Hanging

If you like the look of a large spiral of yarn, you can make a delightful wall hanging using yarn and a paper plate.

You will need:

- Tacky glue.

- Pencil.

- Ruler.

- Paper plate.

- Flat artist brushes.

- Scraps of yarn.

- Scissors.

- Hanging bracket.

- Hot glue.

First, find the center of the paper plate using a ruler. Draw a vertical line through the center. Switch the ruler to a horizontal position in the middle of the plate and draw another line. The place where the two lines meet is the center of the plate. Cut strands of yarn in random lengths, between two and six inches long. You can combine any yarn colors you wish or stick to a single shade.

Paint a circle of glue onto the center of the plate. Put some glue on the beginning of a strand of yarn, stick it in the middle of the plate, and tightly wind it in a spiral around and around. Keep the yarn tight; you don't want to see any plate between the strands of yarn. Whenever you reach the end of a piece of yarn, add a little glue to the end before you stick it onto the plate. Do the same with the start of the next piece, and continue to follow the curve around the plate. Keep going, adding strands of yarn until you reach the edge of the plate.

You will notice that the edges of the plate will bow in. This is perfectly normal; it adds extra depth to the piece. Let the piece dry overnight. NOTE: If you do not want the backside of the plate on the bowing rim to appear white, you can always paint it with acrylics prior to gluing. I created a plate using shades of green. Instead of letting the white show, I painted the back rim of my plate forest green.

Attach a hanging bracket to a flat back section of the plate; then it will be ready to grace your wall.

Woven Butterfly

These butterflies look nice hanging in windows or on the refrigerator, with the help of magnets.

You will need:

- Craft sticks.

- Pipe cleaners.

- Yarn in several colors.

- Small beads.

- 1 large bead.

Make an "X" with the sticks and start winding yarn around them near the middle, crossing over the sticks to hold them in place. When the sticks are secure, wind the yarn in a figure eight along two of the sticks, changing color whenever you wish. When the yarn approaches the end, stop and knot it. Do the same with the other "wings."

Fold a pipe cleaner in half and twist the bottom at the fold. String two small beads on over the fold and secure it by bending the fold up. Take one side of the pipe cleaner behind the wings in the middle and the other in front. Twist the pipe cleaner at the top. Thread both ends of the pipe cleaner through the large bead and twist it again above the top of the bead to make the head of the butterfly. Separate the ends of the pipe cleaner to each side of the head and curl them up to create the butterfly's antennae.

Yarn Basket

Yarn baskets are nice looking and when you get the hang of wrapping the yarn tightly around the clothesline, you can probably sell these at craft shows. These are very sturdy; they can hold fruit as well as other moderately heavy items.

You will need:

- Yarn.

- Clothesline (I prefer brown clothesline so that the color doesn't show through as easily).

- Yarn needles.

- Scissors.

Cut six feet of yarn. Hold the end of the clothesline in your left hand to the left and the yarn end about one inch from the end of the clothesline going in the opposite direction. Bend the end of the yarn in half, hold it against the clothesline, and wrap it tightly, so that none of the clothesline shows through. Keep wrapping until you reach the end of the yarn, then bend the yarn up to make a loop and wrap it at the base of the loop. This is the center bottom of the basket. Thread a smaller piece of yarn in the needle and secure it with two stitches in the middle of the loop.

Keep cutting and wrapping yarn. When enough has been wrapped, coil around that loop and secure it with two stitches every so often. This makes the bottom of the basket. Start coiling wrapped clothesline up the sides and stitching until you have shaped your basket as you prefer.

Yarn Bowl

Yarn bowls are made in a similar manner as yarn globes, but you don't put yarn over the entire sphere. These bowls are pretty; although they should not be immersed in water, they are very versatile as display containers. You can use them to hold a collection of yarn globes; they can also be used to collect change, jewelry, or other small items around the house.

You will need:

- 1 bowl the size of your yarn bowl. Metal and glass bowls work really well because the plastic wrap sticks well to them. Plastic bowls might be a problem.

- Plastic wrap.

- School glue.

- Water.

- Container to mix glue.

- Yarn .

- Scissors.

Protect your work surface with newspaper or plastic, because this project is very messy. Turn the bowl you upside down and cover the dome and sides with plastic wrap. Mix glue and water in a three-to-one ratio in a container. It should not be too watery. Cut strands of yarn into easily managed lengths and immerse them in the glue solution. After soaking for a few minutes, pinch an end and run the yarn through your fingers to remove excess solution from the yarn. Then wind it back and forth and around the outside of the bowl.

Keep wrapping until the dome of the bowl is covered. Press the yarn gently with hands so everything is smooth, then let it dry in place for 24 hours. After everything is completely dry, lift your yarn up off the bowl and carefully peel off the plastic wrap. Your bowl is now ready for use.

Yarn Dolls

Yarn dolls add color to a room and joy to children.

Yarn dolls have been made and loved for centuries. Little girls really did play with these dolls ages ago. They still make delightful embellishments to light switches and can add charm to a room by hanging from handles of cupboards or from window latches.

You will need:

- Yarn.

- Scissors.

- Yarn needle.

- 4 by 6 inch index card pack.

An unopened pack of four by six index cards makes a perfectly sized yarn doll. Wrap the yarn about 100 times around the short side of the cards. Cut the yarn off. Also, cut an eight-inch strand of yarn. Take the wrapped yarn off the card stack and wrap the eight inch piece around the top loop to make a head. Tie it in a knot and let the excess hang down with the rest of the yarn.

Cut another eight-inch piece of yarn and thread it in a yarn needle. Insert the needle in the top center of the head and back up, as if you were making a stitch. Tie the ends together in a knot to give you a loop from which to hang your yarn doll. You now have a head and an uncut tassel-like object. Take your scissors and cut the bottom to free the yarn so you do have a big tassel. Separate the body yarn (tassel) into three groups; one big one in the middle and two smaller ones on either side.

Cut another strand of yarn and bring it under the two smaller bundles so they do not get caught and tie a waist in your yarn doll. Cut two smaller pieces of yarn and tie the two smaller bundles at the end to make arms. Hold the doll by the head and even out the yarn at the bottom if necessary. You now have a girl doll with a dress. If you want to make it boy doll, just separate the bottom yarn into two sections and tie at bottom of each leg with two more strands of yarn.

Yarn Globes

These globes are easy to make and look lovely in a basket, wooden bowl, or glass dish.

You will need:

- 4- to 5-inch diameter round balloons.

- School glue.

- Water.

- Bowl.

- Plastic spoon.

- Scissors.

- Yarn.

Blow up the balloons to the desired size. You might want to vary the sizes, to make the grouping more interesting. Mix three parts glue to one part water in a bowl and stir well with your plastic spoon. It should still be somewhat thick. If you want the finished product to shimmer in the light, you can stir in some glitter.

The next part gets a little messy, so have paper towels ready. I suggest you put down paper or plastic to protect your work surface.

Cut several six-foot long pieces of yarn. Place them, one at a time, in the bowl with the glue and let them set there, soaking up the glue. When they are well saturated, pick up an end, hold it between your thumb and index finger, and pull with the other fingers to remove the excess glue. Place the end against the balloon and start wrapping it loosely around the balloon, creating a web-like design on the balloon. Tuck the ends under another strand to hide them. You can use as much or as little yarn on each balloon as you wish.

When you're happy with your yarn work, cut a 12-inch piece of yarn and wind it around the knot of the balloon, tying it into a loop. This will allow you to hang the balloon to dry. Hang it over a shower rod or a curtain rod for 24 to 48 hours, allowing the yarn to stiffen. After this time, if the balloon has not already deflated, cut off the knot and pull the balloon out of the yarn, removing it completely, along with the hanging loop.

Yarn Wall Hanging

This wall hanging is fringy and looks beautiful when the wind comes through the house to ruffle the fringe.

You will need:

- Yarn. Use a single color of yarn or vary the colors, as you wish.

- Scissors.

- Cardboard.

- Superglue.

- 7-inch-long wooden dowel rod.

- 1 1/2-inch metal ring.

Cut a four-foot strand of yarn and fold it in half. Put the folded part through the metal ring, then take the ends and put them through the resulting loop, so that it catches the ring. Pull this down to secure with the ring in the middle of the yarn piece. This will give you two ends. Tie each end to either side of the dowel, about a half inch from the end. Saturate each knot with superglue so it will hold. This is your hanger piece.

Cut a piece of cardboard 14 inches wide and about six inches long. Wrap the yarn 10 times around the 14-inch side and cut it from the skein. Cut the resulting loops evenly on one end, so that the yarn hangs free. Fold the bunch in half, pull the loose ends through in a knot, catching the dowel rod this time. Then, tighten the knot. Repeat this process until you have covered the dowel rod with bunches of yarn hanging in fringes. Hang this from the metal ring and trim the ends straight or asymmetrically, as you wish.

Yarn Wall Hanging 2

This wall hanging is similar to the one above except you do not use a dowel rod. In this case you will use a large embroidery hoop.

Create the fringed yarn bunches as above, attaching them to the bottom of the hoop. There is no need to use an attached metal ring to hang it on the wall, however, because the top of the loop will catch onto a nail or hook to hang.

Yarn-Wrapped Desk Accessories

These are the standard desk accessories made from tin cans. You can hold pens and pencils in empty soup cans; empty tuna cans easily and colorfully tame your paperclips. You can also use yarn-wrapped cans to organize crochet and knitting needles, scissors, and other items necessary for these crafts.

You will need:

- Empty cans with labels removed.

- Tacky glue.

- Flat artist's paintbrush.

- Scissors.

- Toothpick.

This is a good project for using variegated yarn, but it can also look attractive when you use a solid color for the entire can. You can introduce strips of a contrasting color at top and bottom, or change colors as many times as you want, creating multiple stripes. You are only limited by your imagination; that, and the extent of your yarn collection!

Start by brushing a thin layer of glue over the entire can, from the top rim down. Add a little extra glue to the tip of your yarn and attach it to the top of the rim, letting a bit of the tail end run down the can. Wrap the unstretched yarn around the can, covering the glued-down tail. With each lap of yarn, touch the previous lap around the can. Use a toothpick to push the yarn next to the previous strand of yarn; you don't want any metal showing through. Change colors as often as you like, overlapping each end and applying a bit of glue to both old and new ends. Wrap your yarn all the way to the bottom rim of the can, then add extra glue to the ending tip of yarn to help it hold.

Let the can dry for 24 hours. You can add depth and interest to your can art if you wish by creating spirals or squares of yarn on top of the original layer. Use contrasting colors if you wish.

Yarn-Wrapped Flowerpot

Wrapping yarn around flowerpots adds color and texture.

These flowerpots are whimsical and look striking indoors with the right plants. I would not put them outdoors; if they get wet the yarn may fall off.

I have my African violets arranged in wrapped pots of variegated purple yarn.

You will need:

- Terra cotta pots.

- Yarn.

- Tacky glue.

- Sponge brush.

- Scissors.

A sponge brush works much better a regular brush in this instance; the pots are porous and will absorb some of the glue. Always leave the rim untouched. This will create a water barrier to protect the yarn.

Start right under the rim and spread glue in a one or two-inch band from the rim down. Put a bit of glue on the beginning end of your yarn and stick it to the pot immediately below the rim. Start winding and sticking so that none of the pot shows through. Keep going until you reach the bottom of the pot. Whenever you need to add another piece of yarn, put a little glue on the tip and place it where the last one ended.

To create an ombre effect, start with dark yarn and gradually shift to lighter shades as you proceed down the pot.

Chapter 12: Kid-Friendly Family Crafts

Doing crafts with your kids makes for a fun time and more. When you do crafts together you help your child learn to follow direction, you develop communication skills with your children, you enhance the creative side of their brains and you deepen relationships as a whole family. The following crafts range from simple items that even a child can make to a little more complicated crafts for toddlers and school-aged kids.

Button Tree Canvas For Kids

This makes a great hanging for hallways.

You will need:

- Canvas.

- Acrylic paint and foam brush.

- Tacky glue.

- Twigs that are mostly flat.

- Colorful buttons.

Paint the canvas like the sky and grass and let it dry. Glue branches and twigs on the canvas to create a trunk and tree branches. If the tacky glue does not work, have an adult firmly affix it with hot glue. Use the tacky glue to attach colorful buttons as leaves. Let the piece dry before hanging it up.

Clay Flowers

Celebrate spring by making cute clay flowers to set on shelves or tables.

You will need:

- Flower cookie cutter or cardboard template.

- Air-drying clay.

- Food coloring.

- Disposable gloves or plastic sandwich bag.

- Green jumbo paper clips.

- Rolling pin.

- Wax paper.

If your air-dry clay is not colored, put it in a closeable bag, add some food coloring, and knead it until the color is thoroughly mixed in. You will need at least three different colors of clay: green, a petal color, and a color for the center of the flower.

Place the flower petal clay on a sheet of wax paper and roll it out to about a half-inch thick. Use a cookie cutter or a butter knife to cut out a small flower shape.

Roll out the clay for the flower's center a little thinner. Cut out the center of the flower and stick it in the center of the flower. Make a small star of green clay to serve as the sepal or base for your flower.

Place the bottom of the large green paper clip (the end with just one wire) into the center of the sepal and press it down far enough that it stays put. Set the flower on the top of the sepal and press it down carefully. Let the flower dry and make more until you have a garden to populate a shelf or decorate a table.

Coffee Filter Ornamental Bowls

These bowls look like stained glass and are easy to make.

You will need:

- Paper coffee filters.

- Scissors.

- Non-permanent markers.

- Plastic cup.

- Spray starch.

Cut the edges of the coffee filter, making it slightly jagged and uneven for interest. Use the markers to give it some color. Mark dots, blobs, or any shapes you like. The ink will spread a little, but that's okay.

Drape the coffee filter over the lip of a plastic cup. If the cup falls over, put some dried beans in the cup for ballast. Spray the coffee filter with spray starch until it is thoroughly wet. The ink will spread when you do this. Let it dry. The coffee filter bowl will retain its shape when removed from the cup and it will be stiff. The colors will have run together to create a stained-glass effect.

Craft Stick Frame

These are easy for kids to make; they can even include a photo of themselves inside.

You will need:

- Regular sized craft sticks.

- Tacky glue.

- Acrylic paint and brush or foam brush.

- Stick on jewels/buttons.

- Hot glue and glue gun (for a slower project, you can use wood glue).

- Ribbon.

- Scissors.

Glue 11 craft sticks close together to make a square. Secure them by gluing four sticks across them all, two at the top and two at the bottom. Let the glue dry completely. Paint the frame as well as four more sticks. You can leave the wood plain if you desire.

Once everything is dry, glue the painted sticks onto the frame. Two will go on the sides and two will go on the stick that is already on the top and bottom. There will be a gap on the sides that will allow you to insert a photo. You might want to put a ring of tape on the back of the photo to hold it in.

To hang the frame on the wall, cut a three-inch piece of ribbon and have an adult hot glue the ends to the top back of the frame, centering it so the frame hangs properly. You can add additional ornamentation by gluing on jewels or buttons, if you wish.

Clothespin Clamps

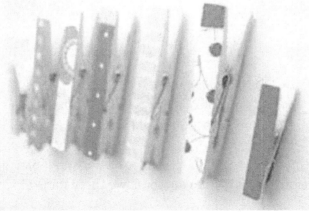

Washi tape adds color to clothespins.

Use alligator clothespins to make clamps to keep chips and pretzel bags shut. These make wonderful gifts for grandparents and aunts or uncles.

You will need:

- Alligator wooden clothespins.

- Washi tape.

- Mod Podge and foam brush.

- Acrylic paint and brush to put it on (optional).

If you want to paint the clothespins, do so first and let them dry. The nice thing about alligator-style clothespins is that they are usually the same width or just a tiny bit wider than washi tape. Cut a piece of washi tape that will fit from the top of the clip to the very end of the clothespin. Stick it on. Cover with a thin layer of Mod Podge to keep the washi tape from peeling off. To use your new clip, fold the top of a bag of chips down and clip it for a good seal.

Clothespin Car Air Fresheners

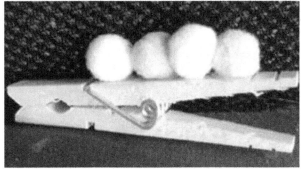

Simple But Functional Car Air Freshener

These clip onto your car vents and make the car smell nice and fresh. You can paint the clothespins if you want or leave them natural.

You will need:

- Alligator-style wooden clothespins.

- Acrylic paint and brush (optional).

- Small pompoms.

- Fragrance or essential oils.

- Eye dropper.

- Tacky glue.

Take three small pompoms and glue them with tacky glue to the very top of the alligator clothespin. Let the glue dry completely. Add a drop of fragrance or essential oil to each pompom. Clip the clothespin on the vent of your car and enjoy the fragrance.

Felt Flower Bookmark

You will need:
- Felt sheets with sticky backs.

- Pen or marker.

- Jumbo plastic-covered paper clips, green in color.

- Scissors.

Draw two flower shapes on the back of the felt and cut them out. Remove the felt backing and stick the flowers together, with the top part of the paper clip between them. You can now fasten the bottom of the paper clip over the pages of a book.

Foam Shape Wreath

You can make a wreath each holiday or you can make a wreath with images that have special meaning to you and your children. For example, a friend helped her children make individual wreaths for the outside of their bedroom doors. Her son loved baseball, so they included a baseball, a ball diamond, and bat shapes to decorate the wreath. Her daughter loved ponies, so her wreath was full of pony shapes.

You will need:

- Foam shapes or sheets of foam with adhesive on the back.

- Pencil.

- Template.

- Scissors.

- Tacky glue (for non-adhesive foam).

- Paper plates.

Cut the middle out of a paper plate, leaving only the rim. Set aside. If you are using sheets of foam, use a cardboard template to make shapes on the back of the sheet, tracing it with a pencil. Cut out these shapes.

Place the paper plate face down on a flat surface Peel the paper from the back of the foam shapes and stick them onto the rim, overlapping them slightly so that none of the paper plate rim is showing. If your shapes lack an adhesive back, put some tacky glue on the back of each shape and stick them to the rim of the plate. Then be careful to let the glue dry before proceeding.

Once all the shapes are attached, you can add ribbon, paper curls, or other ornamentation if you like. The wreath will hang on a door if a hook catches the inner rim of the plate.

Glove Monsters

I love these little monsters. They are much more cute than scary. This craft teaches older kids the basics of sewing on a machine.

You will need:

- Colorful winter gloves.

- Polyester fiberfill.

- Sewing machine and thread.

- Needle and thread.

- Buttons, yarn, ribbon, silk flowers, and other enhancements.

Turn the glove inside out and sew a "U" shape from the top of the thumb-hole to the other side of the glove, leaving a one inch diameter hole at the top where the hand normally goes into the glove. Turn the glove right side out and stuff it with fiberfill. Put plenty of fiberfill in the fingers to prevent them from drooping.

Tuck the cuff, where the stuffing hole is, to the inside and hand stitch it shut. Stitch buttons on for eyes and nose, then stitch a ribbon on to make a mouth. Do whatever you want to make your monster unique.

Handprint Salt Clay Bird

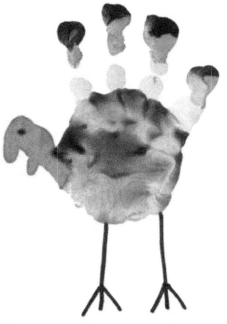

Painted Handprint Bird

This craft uses a child's handprint to create a little knick-knack for grandma and grandpa's tables. Because of the palm imprint, it can hold rings or small change.

You will need:

- Salt clay (See the recipe in sculpture section).

- Rolling pin.

- Wax paper.

- Knife.

- Acrylic paint and a brush.

- Glitter.

- Parchment paper.

- Cookie sheet.

Roll the salt clay out on wax paper until it is about three quarters of an inch thick. Press the child's outstretched hand into the clay to make a deep impression. Place the clay on a cookie sheet covered with parchment paper.

You will be using the child's hand to create a bird. The head of the bird is the thumb. Pinch a little piece of clay where the thumbnail was to make a beak. Bake the clay in a 250-degree Fahrenheit oven for one to two hours until it is hard. Let it cool completely. Paint the hand with acrylic paint that has a little glitter added.

Knot Ring

Kids love to wear these cute little knot rings; you can make one for Mom or grandma too. You can locate the base for the ring in the "findings" area of a craft store's jewelry department.

You will need:

- Base ring finding, adjustable.

- E6000 glue. Keep the kids from getting this on themselves, because it takes alcohol to remove the stuff!

- Old t-shirt.

- Scissors.

Cut the hem off the t-shirt and cut a thin strip about a half-inch wide and eight inches long. It will curl, but don't worry about that. Make a knot in the middle of the strip and keep making knots until you have reached the end of the fabric.

Bunch the knots together and glue them onto the ring base with the E6000 glue. Let it dry. You can do this with ribbon too; you'll need 10 to 12 inches of the stuff.

Magazine People

This is a fun project for families with little kids. You make faces from magazine cut outs and put them up on the refrigerator with magnets.

You will need:

- Old magazines.

- Scissors.

- School glue.

- Paper.

- Markers.

Have the kids cut eyes, noses, mouths, ears, hair, and clothing from magazine pictures. The object is to draw a head and glue everything on to make a magazine person. Make them as outrageous or as beautiful as you like.

Magic Wands

Every little girl wants a pretty magic wand. In this project, you will use craft sticks to make one.

You will need:

- Craft sticks.

- Acrylic paint and foam brush.

- Stick on jewels.

- Foam star stickers; alternatively, you can cut out your own stars by wielding scissors on a foam sheet. For these, you'll need spray adhesive.

Paint the craft sticks and let them dry. Stick two stars together with the craft stick in between at the bottom. If you make your own stars, spray the inside with spray adhesive and stick them together, with the craft stick inside at the bottom. Add stick on jewels up the craft stick and you have a wand.

Paper Bead Necklace

Paper beads make a light and elegant necklace.

Paper beads are fun to make out of magazine pictures that are colorful or from black and white newsprint. You can also use scrapbook paper.

You will need:

- Scissors.

- Scrapbook paper or colorful pages from magazines.

- Bamboo skewer.

- Glue stick.

- Mod Podge and foam brush or acrylic spray.

- Wax paper.

- String for necklace.

Cut the magazine pages or scrapbook paper into long skinny triangles. Starting with the wide end, wrap the triangle around the skewer, keeping point in the center of the elongated bead. The skewer forms a hole in the bead so it can be strung later. With the last inch of the paper, wipe it with a glue stick and wrap it tightly around to fasten the paper down. If you cut similar-sized triangles, your beads will end up about the same size.

Let the glue dry before painting each bead with Mod Podge or covering it with acrylic spray on first one side. Let it dry thoroughly before treating the opposite side. After everything is dry, string your beads together to make a necklace.

Pet Bugs

Make your own pet bugs out of clear gems that have a flat bottom and a dome on top. These are also called clear cabochons and are found in the jewelry aisle of a craft store.

You will need:

- Clear gems.

- Pencil.

- Scrapbook paper scraps.

- Scissors.

- Google eyes.

- Clear glue that is safe for kids.

Place the flat part of the clear gem on the back of the scrapbook paper and trace around it with the pencil. Cut the form out just a little smaller than the tracing. Put some clear glue on the flat bottom of the gem and stick the colorful part of the cut out scrapbook paper against the glued bottom. The colorful paper will show through to the top of the gem. Press it down to affix the glue and wipe away any excess. Let it dry. Glue some google eyes onto the top of the bug.

Picture Frame Sun-Catcher

These sun-catchers can radiate color throughout a room, adding warmth and interest to the environment.

You will need:

- Cheap picture frames with glass centers.

- Plastic condiment bottles.

- Paper glue.

- Neon-colored liquid food coloring.

- Hot glue and glue gun.

- Sheet of white paper.

- Super glue and suction cups (optional).

Take the backing off the frames and discard them. Hot glue the glass to the frame on the inside. Run a bead of hot glue along where the glass meets the frame. The object is to prevent the paint from leaking out through the edges.

Set the frame face down on the table with white paper underneath. The white paper makes it easy to see what you are doing. Fill the condiment bottles with white glue mixed with food coloring. Shake before using and make designs on the inside of the glass. Make a spiral, a rainbow or anything else. It will all run together anyway. Don't use too many colors or they can easily blend and turn into a muddy brown mess.

Let the project dry for several days, depending on the thickness of the glue mixture. When everything is completely dry, clean off any errant glue spots and either prop the frame up against a window or hot glue suction cups to the four corners of the frame and stick it on the window.

Polymer Clay Key Chain

Polymer Clay Key ring

Roll your polymer clay out to half an inch thick. Cut out shapes or mold whatever form suits you. You can use a rubber stamp to mark a design or an initial into the clay before baking. Spread Mod Podge over the clay after baking to protect it from chipping. Hook your finished product onto a key chain using a jump ring. .

Polymer Clay Window Ornaments

Roll these out thin and hang them in a window to let the sun shine through.

You will need:

- Several colors of polymer clay.

- Pasta machine used only for clay.

- Wax paper.

- Cookie cutters.

- Skewer.

- Baking sheet covered with parchment paper.

- String or narrow ribbon.

Combine the polymer clay by making logs, placing them side by side and on top of one another and twisting or by other methods of combining polymer clay to make a colorful display. Keep your mixing to a minimum, to avoid muddying the colors.

Pull off a handful of clay, flatten it, then put it through the pasta machine to create a thin sheet. You may need to process your sheet through the machine several times until it is a quarter inch thick. Lay this on some wax paper and use cookie cutters to cut out shapes. Use a wooden skewer to make a hole in the top of each shape from which the figure will hang.

Place the shapes on a cookie sheet covered with parchment paper and bake them per the package instructions. Watch them carefully so that they don't turn brown. Remove the cookie sheet from the oven and let the shapes cool to room temperature. Thread a piece of string or ribbon through the hole and tie it in a loop. Your ornaments are now ready to hang in the window for all to enjoy.

Rainbow Suncatcher

The tissue paper in this project catches the sun and throws color all over the room. Hang this in a window to get full effect.

You will need:

- Tissue paper in several colors.

- Scissors.

- Foam brush.

- Clear sheet protector.

- Mod Podge.

Cut pieces of tissue paper in one-by-one-inch squares. Cut the sheet protector in half to give you two full sheets. Spread a layer of Mod Podge over the sheet protector and stick the tissue paper to it. Paint over the tissue paper with more Mod Podge and let it dry.

Cut the sheet protector in the shape of a heart, star, triangle, or another shape. Bend it so that the colored tissue paper will peel away from it. Punch a hole in the top and thread yarn through the hole to hang it in the window.

Rainstick

The Original Rainstick, Made From Cactus

Rainsticks make a delightful trickling sound when they are turned and you can make your own out of a cardboard tube from aluminum foil or plastic wrap. You can also use a wrapping paper tube.

You will need:

- Cardboard tube.

- Tempera or acrylic paint and paintbrush.

- Brown paper from a grocery bag.

- Yarn.

- Rubber bands.

- Scissors.

- Pipe cleaners.

- Dry rice.

- Dry beans.

Paint the tubes to look like wood, using brown paint with tan and white streaks. Let the paint dry thoroughly before proceeding. Cut two circles from grocery bags about two inches larger than the opening of the tube. Crumple both circles and flatten them out to give them a worn look. Attach one circle over one end of the tube, holding it firmly with rubber bands. Cut a fringe, using the excess paper below the rubber bands; just don't cut through the rubber bands themselves.

Half-fill the tube with dry beans and rice. Take a few pipe cleaners, twist them a few times, and put them in as well. The rice and beans will catch on the pipe cleaners and gradually fall down the tube. Attach the other paper circle to the other end and do the same with the rubber band and fringe. Tie colored pieces of yarn over both the rubber bands and you're finished. Tip the rain stick over to make it sound like rain.

Sun Catcher Lids

Another idea for a window sun catcher is to use plastic lids from butter, sour cream, or other food items. You can use any size of lid.

You will need:

- Plastic lids.

- Paper glue.

- Food coloring.

- Toothpicks.

- Hole punch.

- Ribbon.

Pour enough glue into a plastic lid to cover the entire surface. Scatter a few drops of two to four different food colors on the glue. Take a toothpick, insert it into the glue, and swirl it around to make interesting patterns with the colors. Let the glue dry for three days. At this point, the edges will start to separate and peel from the lid.

Once the glue is completely dry, peel off the colored glue from the lid. Punch a hole in the top of the glue, run a ribbon through the hole, and tie it in a loop. Hang your sun catcher in the window where it will be sure to catch the sun's rays.

Tic Tac Tote

This is a ready-to-go game that you can take with you anywhere.

You will need:

- A small drawstring bag.

- Small flat stones.

- Fabric paint in a squeeze bottle.

- Acrylic paint and brush.

This bag stores your playing pieces until you need them.

Paint two vertical lines and cross them with two horizontal lines to make a tic-tac-toe board, using fabric paint on the flat surface of the bag. Set this aside to dry. With nine rocks paint a white "X" on one side and let it dry. Turn the stones over and paint a white "O" on the other side. Let the paint dry, then use the bag as the board and store the stones in the bag.

Tin Can Mobile

Tin cans can make a pleasant sound when they collide in a breeze. This mobile looks great hung on your front porch or in the garden.

You will need:

- 5 or 6 tin cans of different sizes with the labels removed. .

- Acrylic paint.

- Foam brush.

- Painter's tape.

- Hammer.

- Nail.

- Twine scissors.

- 10-inch embroidery hoop.

- Hot glue and glue gun.

- Clear acrylic spray.

Paint the cans, giving them two coats of base paint. Once they are dry, paint designs on them. Use painter's tape as desired to create stripes and other shapes. Remove the tape after the paint is dry.

Turn the cans upside down and set a nail against the center of the bottom. Tap gently with a hammer to make a small hole in the bottom of each can. Cut three to five inches of twine and thread it through the hole of the cans making a knot on the inside. Place a few drops of hot glue on the knot and pull it taut.

Tie these strings to the embroidery hoop, spacing the cans evenly around the hoop. Cut three two-foot pieces of twine and tie it on either side of the hoop then bring the twine together and tie it in a single knot at the top to hang it.

Twig Frame

This project is for older kids who know how to use a glue gun. The twigs should be smaller in diameter than a pencil.

You will need:

- A small, cheap, wooden frame.

- Twigs from a tree (a lot of them).

- Hot glue and glue gun.

- Spray adhesive (optional).

- Glitter or fake snow (optional).

Remove the glass from the frame, if it exists, and set it aside in a safe place. Take handfuls of twigs in a bundle and start hot gluing them around the frame in an orderly manner. Start at a bottom corner and glue on twigs around the frame, until most of the frame is covered. Let the glue dry.

You can leave the frame as is or you can add a festive look by applying some spray adhesive and sprinkling on glitter or fake snow. When you're finished, just return the glass to the frame, insert a photo, and hang it on the wall.

Wooden Utensils, Decorated

Painted utensils add joy to life.

Liven up those old wooden spoons in your kitchen. Wooden utensils are inexpensive and the wood is untreated; this makes it easy to apply some paint or washi tape to the handles. The only trick is, you have to apply the decorations near the top of the utensils because acrylic paint will wash off, as will washi tape. The Mod Podge will only protect it to a certain degree.

You will need:

- Wooden utensils.

- Acrylic paint and paintbrush or washi tape and scissors.

- Sandpaper, if painting.

- Mod Podge and foam brush.

If painting, sand the handles lightly to ensure that they are completely smooth. Wipe them off well with a dry cloth. Paint no lower than a couple inches above the bowl of the spoon. You can decorate them using stripes, pictures, dots or whatever you like. If you are using washi tape, you can use stripes, spirals, or any other configuration you can imagine. Once the paint has dried or the washi tape is applied, cover your work with a layer of Mod Podge. Let this dry completely before you use it.

Chapter 13: Holiday Crafts

Holiday crafts are fun for the whole family to make. You can make them as decorations for any of the holidays you celebrate as a family. Kids of all ages enjoy playing together when it comes to making holiday crafts. After all, what's more fun than being able to tell guests, "I helped make that"?

When most people think of the word "holiday," Christmas comes to mind. There are several Christmas crafts in this chapter. However, our world is highly diversified when it comes to holidays. You can find crafts here for each of them. Explore the decorating ideas that follow for Halloween, Thanksgiving, Hanukkah, Valentine's Day, St. Patrick's Day, and Easter. Now, you can have year-round fun making holiday crafts.

Burlap Silverware Holders

I love these silverware and napkin holders. They look like a little envelope into which you slide the napkin and silverware for each place setting. If you have a buffet, it is easy for guests to pick up their little burlap envelope and carry it to the table with their plates.

You will need:

- 4-inch-wide wired burlap ribbon.

- Hot glue and glue gun.

- Fabric paint pen.

- Raffia.

- Scissors.

- Wire cutters.

Use the wire cutters to cut the wire part of the burlap ribbon in a 12-inch strip. Fold it up at the bottom about four and a half inches; glue along the sides to make a little envelope with a long open upper side. Use the fabric pen to write names, or any other word like "Blessings," "Thanks" or "Eat" on the front folded part. Insert a napkin first and lay the silverware on top. Tie a piece of raffia around the top flap and the silverware, making a bow.

Button Christmas Tree

You will need green buttons in a variety of shapes and sizes, but they should be flat with four holes. You can use a few brown and tan ones for the trunk.

You will need:

- Buttons.

- Clear filament.

- 1 small jump ring.

- Scissors.

- Ribbon.

- Needle-nose pliers.

- Star charm for top (optional).

Sort buttons from small to large. Cut 20 inches of clear filament. When you string up the buttons you'll want to bring the filament up through one of the four holes on one side and down another on the other side so the button is in the middle of the filament and fastened snugly. Do this with the large brown or tan button for the base of the trunk. String on several more brown buttons to flesh out the trunk. I used about five brown buttons on the ornament I made.

Once the brown buttons are in place, attach the largest green button then and string more green ones, getting smaller and smaller until you have created the size of tree you want. Mine was three inches in height. Add the star charm if desired and knot the filament at the top so it is very tight.

Take any excess filament and force it down through the buttons, cutting any that won't fit.

Pull a jump ring apart with the needle-nose pliers and insert one end into the loop made by the knot in the filament. Close the jump ring. Cut a piece of ribbon and insert it through the jump ring, tying it together to form a loop.

Canning Ring Pumpkin

Make this dynamic Halloween or Thanksgiving decoration with canning rings (the part that screws on the canning jar). These instructions have you paint the lids, but you can leave them plain, too.

You will need:

- About 20 canning rings of the same size.

- Spray paint in orange, black, or white.

- 4 four-inch-long cinnamon sticks.

- Scissors.

- String, twine, or yarn.

- Hot glue.

Spray paint the rings if desired, on both sides, and let them dry. Make sure all the rings are facing the same direction and pull a length of string, twine, or yarn through them to tie the rings together. Pull the string tight and make a knot. Gently slip the lids over the string to form a circular, pumpkin shape. There will be a sizeable hole in the middle. Hot glue a bundle of cinnamon sticks together and insert this in the center hole to serve as a fragrant stem.

Clothespin Turkeys

Use the alligator-type wooden clothespins to make this cute turkey craft for fall decorating or Thanksgiving.

You will need:

- Clothespins.

- Fake fall leaves in fall colors.

- 1 inch diameter circle punch.

- Brown cardstock.

- Yellow and red construction paper.

- Small google eyes.

- Tacky glue.

- Scissors.

These directions are for making one turkey.

Punch one hole, the head, from card stock and glue on the google eyes. Cut a small square of yellow construction paper and fold it in half diagonally for the beak; glue it on the head. Cut a small teardrop shape out of red construction paper to make the turkey's wattle and glue it under the beak.

Glue the head to the top of the clothespin. The top is where you press down to make the clothespin open. The jaws will hold the leaf tail up on top. The underside of the turkey is the flat side. After gluing, the jaws of the clothespin are on top, so the head has to face away from the top. Cut the stem from the leaf and clip it in the clothespin jaws so the leaf is upright above the head.

OPTIONS: you can apply Thanksgiving or fall motif washi tape to the top of the clothespin above the head going toward the jaws. Then glue a strip magnet to the underside of the turkey to attach it to your refrigerator.

Craft Stick Halloween Spider

Even little kids can make these scary spiders; they're fun to set on tables or tape to walls.

You will need:

- Regular craft sticks.

- Hot glue and glue gun or tacky glue.

- Black and white felt.

- Scissors.

- Black acrylic paint.

- Paintbrush or foam brush.

Paint both the front and the back of four craft sticks with black paint and let them dry. Make eyes from felt by cutting out two one-inch-diameter white circles and two half-inch-diameter black circles. Use tacky glue to affix the black circles to the white circles. Cut a three-inch-diameter circle from black felt to serve as the body of the spider.

Make a skinny "X" with two of the craft sticks and glue these together with hot glue or tacky glue (hot glue is preferred). Make a wider "X" with the other two craft sticks and glue them together. Glue the two groupings of craft sticks together so that the spider will have four legs on one side of the intersection and four legs on the other side. Glue the body on in the middle of the craft sticks. Add the eyes and you have a spider with which to startle your friends.

Craft Stick Star Of David

Popsicle Stick Star of David

Make individual stars and hang them around the home to decorate for Hanukkah. You can also make a garland by connecting several stars with waxed cotton string running through the side arms of the stars. This looks best attached over a door or hanging from a mantle.

You will need:

- Regular craft sticks.

- Acrylic paint and brushes (I used blue and white paint).

- Hot glue and glue gun.

- Stick-on jewels.

Paint three craft sticks blue and three craft sticks white, letting one side dry before turning the sticks over and painting the other side. Be careful to paint the edges as well. Glue the blue sticks together to form a triangle and make a second triangle with the white sticks. Place the blue triangle on a flat protected surface with the point down. Glue a white triangle onto the blue one with the point of the triangle pointing up; this will complete the six-sided Star of David. Let the glue dry before adding ornamentation in the form of stick-on jewels to each point and juncture of the triangles.

Delicate Designs On Dyed Easter Eggs

Dying Easter eggs is a tradition in many households. In this case, you will use fabric to create delicate designs on the dyed eggs.

You will need:

- Hard boiled eggs.

- Easter egg dye.

- Loose woven fabric like lace, burlap, nylon netting, eyelet or cheesecloth.

- Rubber band.

- Scissors.

Wrap a square of fabric around the egg and twist the edge tightly so the fabric is tightly against the egg, without breaking the shell. Secure this with a rubber band and dunk the egg in the dye. Let the egg dry and remove the fabric. The imprint of the fabric will remain on the egg, giving it a pretty design.

Easter-inspired Jar

Use this as a vase to hold daffodils or pussy willow branches.

You will need:

- Acrylic paint in pastel colors.

- Foam brush.

- Glass jar.

- Painter's tape.

- 80 grit sandpaper (optional).

Paint two coats of a base paint on the jar, using the foam brush. Let this dry for 24 hours. Use the tape to mask off a design that will remain the base color. Next, you will paint the rest of the jar using another color. If you want the jar to be striped, place the tape around the jar and put several strips evenly spaced down the jar. Paint the second color and let it dry for 24 hours.

Another method is to use a shaped foam brush to paint shapes around the jar. After everything is completely dry, you can remove the painter's tape. You can leave your jars like this or, for a more rustic look, rub it lightly with the sandpaper in several spots to distress the finish. I put some Easter grass in the bottom, a chocolate bunny on top, and some jellybeans and Easter kisses in the middle for a lovely tasty treat.

Easy Homemade Menorah With Glass Votive Candles

If you don't have a menorah, you can easily make your own, using some wrapped boxes and glass votive candles.

You will need:

- 8 small gift boxes.

- 1 slighter larger gift box.

- Wrapping paper.

- Ribbon for wrapping presents.

- A bow for presents.

- Double-sided tape.

- Regular invisible tape.

- Scissors.

- 9 glass votive candle holders with candles.

Wrap the gift boxes and wind a ribbon around each box around the center of each box. Make sure the ribbon lines up as you set the boxes side by side. Tape the wrapped and ribboned boxes together; there should be four setting to one side of the larger box and four on the other side. Use double-sided tape to stick the boxes together.

Attach double-sided tape to the bottom of each votive candleholder and set one on top of each box, centered on the lid. Press down firmly to ensure they stick. Attach the bow to front of the center box and there you have it: your very own menorah!

Egg Carton Easter Containers

Use paper egg cartons instead of Easter baskets this year. Just paint them up, put Easter grass in each compartment, and fill them with candy and little trinkets. Close the lid and there will be a surprise inside.

You will need:

- Paper egg carton.

- Acrylic paint.

- Brushes and foam brush.

Paint the inside of the egg carton, both the bottom and the top, and let it dry. This might take two coats. Turn the carton upside down and paint the outside of the compartments. Let this dry and then paint the top of the lid.

Decorate the top with polka dots, stripes or any other design. You can even paint the name of the child that belongs to this container. Once it is dry, place a little Easter grass in each compartment, and fill the compartments with treats like candy kisses, miniature peanut butter cups, small candies, jellybeans, or small trinkets.

Felt And Button Feather Tree

This ornament resembles an old-fashioned German feather tree with the branches wide on the trunk.

You will need:

- Felt in tan and green.

- Poster board.

- Tacky glue.

- Buttons.

- Thread.

- Needle.

- Embroidery thread.

- Embroidery needle.

Cut the following:

- Tan felt rectangles, five inches long and a half inch wide.

- A poster board rectangle, four and three quarter inches long, and a quarter inch wide.

- Green felt rectangles, one and a half inches by a half inch .

- A piece of poster board, one and a quarter inches by a quarter inch.

- Green felt rectangles, two and a half inches by a half inch.

- A piece of poster board, two and a quarter inches by a quarter inch.

- Green felt rectangles, three and a half inches by a half inch.

- A piece of poster board, three and a quarter inches by a quarter inch.

- Green felt rectangles, four and a half inches by a half inch.

- A piece of poster board, four and a quarter inches by a quarter inch.

Sandwich the poster board pieces inside the corresponding felt pieces and glue them together with the tacky glue. The poster board should set in the middle of each of the felt rectangles to add substance and stiffness. Sew buttons onto one side of the branches with regular thread and needle.

The tan rectangle is the trunk of the tree and the green ones are glued vertically to the trunk at even intervals. Start two inches from the bottom and glue on the longest of the green branches so the trunk is in the middle. Proceed with the rest, getting gradually smaller, with the top one about one to a half inch from the top.

Start at the top of the branch and thread the embroidery needle with two threads of embroidery floss. Sew a whipstitch down to the first branch and around that branch. Insert the needle to come out near the next section of the trunk, then sew to the next branch. Repeat this process all around the tree.

Sew a yellow button to the top of the tree to serve as a star. Glue a loop of embroidery thread to the back of the button so you can hang it.

Firecracker Favors

Kids enjoy receiving these on patriotic holidays, or on any special day. They are filled with candy and little toys, like individual piñatas you don't have to break. I fill mine with small plastic toys, candy kisses in patriotic colors, and crayons. You can make these from toilet paper rolls or – for a sturdier alternative – you can use shipping tubes. 12-inch shipping tubes work best, but you can also cut down 18-inch tubes to size.

You will need:

- Shipping tubes with a plastic top and bottom.

- 12-by-12-inch scrapbook paper with a patriotic design.

- Cupcake picks with foil that looks like firecrackers or a flame. Cupcake picks are toothpicks with a sharp point that goes into the cupcake. Use little flags if you can't find anything else.

- Glue.

- Red and blue pipe cleaners.

- Serrated knife (optional, to cut tubes down to size).

- Ruler.

- Pencil.

- Ice pick or something sharp to poke a hole in the plastic lid.

- Scissors.

- Wire cutters.

- Other embellishments (ribbon, stickers, stick-on jewels).

Cut your tube down to size if necessary, using the serrated knife. Poke a hole in the middle of one of the plastic ends of the tube and set it aside. Leave the other cap on the end. Glue scrapbook paper around the tube and cut off any excess. You may want to roll and mark where the paper meets and remove it from the roll prior to cutting it a little longer. Rewrap the tube and glue the paper down.

Decorate the tube with extra embellishments. Put the bottom cap on the firecracker and fill the tube with goodies. Take the cap with the hole in it and insert one blue pipe cleaner, the cupcake pick and one red pipe cleaner in the hole. Curl the pipe cleaners by wrapping them around a finger. Put the cap on the top of the tube and your firecracker favor is ready.

Ghost In A Jar

These are cute and add a touch of whimsy to a mantle or end table.

You will need:

- 1 large, clear glass jar.

- Glow-in-the-dark spray paint.

- Black spray paint.

- Polyester fiberfill.

- Wire coat hanger or large gauge craft wire.

- Wire cutters.

- Small black beads.

- Glue.

- Paintbrush.

- Air-drying clay.

- Silver scrapbook paper.

- Scissors.

- Black tissue paper.

- Rubber band.

- Black ribbon.

- Paper plate.

- Flameless votive candles (battery operated).

Lightly spray the top and bottom of the jar with black spray paint. You should be able to see inside the jar. Let the paint dry.

Cut an eight-inch piece of wire from the hanger or heavy gauge craft wire. Form this into a frame for your ghost. Stick the ends in a mound of air-dry clay so it will stand upright. It should look like a misshapen loop imbedded in a mound of clay. This can be any size, as long as it fits inside the jar. Let the clay dry before proceeding.

Cover the frame of your ghost with fiberfill and spray it with glow in the dark spray paint. Let this dry. Glue beads to the head of the ghost for eyes and set the ghost in the jar. Cut the silver scrapbook paper to fit behind the ghost in the jar and slide it in. This makes a reflection of the glow in the dark paint and makes the ghost look more ethereal.

Cut a paper plate to fit over the opening of the jar and paint both sides black. Make a hole in the center. This hole will hold the bulb of the flameless votive candle. Place the votive candle over the hole, insert it facedown, and place it over the rim of the jar so that it shines on the ghost. You might have to tape it down, but the plate should be a little larger than the hole, so it doesn't fall in. Cover the plate circle and the opening of the jar with several layers of black tissue paper cut about two inches larger than the opening. Secure these around the rim of the opening with a rubber band and cover the rubber band with ribbon tied in a bow.

You now have a pet ghost. You will need to remove the ribbon, rubber band, and tissue paper to turn the votive on and off.

Holiday Accent Pillow Covers

Instead of changing out your accent pillows for Christmas, make pillowcases that match the current holiday.

You will need:

- Tape measure.

- Holiday fabric/or plain fabric.

- Sewing machine.

- Scissors.

- Thread.

- Pins.

- Fabric paint (optional).

- Iron and ironing board.

Measure the length and width of your accent pillows. Cut two pieces of fabric that are three and a half inches larger than your pillow. For example, if you have a 12-by-12 inch pillow, you would cut two 15 1/2-inch squares of fabric.

You can combine these several different ways. The back can be muslin while the front is a holiday print; you can make them out of the same fabric or you can use plain fabric and paint a festive design on it with fabric paint. Let the paint dry before you proceed.

Pin the two pieces of fabric together with the right sides facing each other inside. Sew three of the sides together and remove the pins. Fold down the open edge a quarter-inch, press it with an iron, and pin it together. Stitch a hem on the sewing machine. Turn the hem down again by one inch and sew it close to the edge.

Turn your pillow cover right side out and place it on the pillow. You can further enhance the festive pillow by sewing ribbon to the open end, about two inches down, before you sew the cover together.

Paint Chip Ornaments

These little paper Christmas trees are delightful and are easily made from paint chips you get at the hardware store. If you ask, the store might have outdated paint chips you can use, instead of pilfering them. For Christmas ornaments you only need chips in shades of green and brown. Of course, you'll want to adjust the color scheme if you want to make these for other holidays

You will need:

- Paint chips in shades of green and brown.

- Scissors.

- Tacky glue.

- Yarn or ribbon.

- Hole punch.

- Colorful paper (optional: scrapbook paper).

- Glitter, star stickers, and thin ribbon (optional).

Using a green paint chip, cut a large narrow triangle the entire length of the chip. This will be a Christmas tree. Cut a rectangle from one of the brown colors to serve as the tree trunk. Glue the trunk to the bottom of the tree. NOTE: If the paint chip has a glossy back, tacky glue will not stick; you'll need to use double-sided tape instead.

Use a hole-punch to cut several circles out of colorful paper. These will become the ornaments for your little green tree. I have also used star stickers for ornaments and thin ribbon as garland. Punch a hole at the top of the tree, insert a piece of ribbon or yarn, and tie a knot to make a hanger.

Paper Heart Valentine's Day Wreath

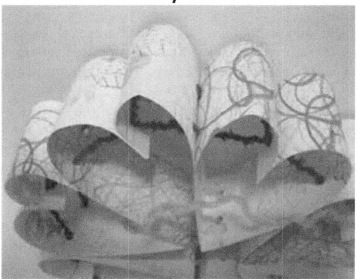

Detail Of Heart Wreath

This wreath makes a great wall decoration; it also looks striking up against a door. You will make heart outlines with paper and fasten them together to create an intriguing wreath.

You will need:

- Cardstock – mine was pink, red and white. You can also use white cardstock and draw whatever you want, keeping in mind that it's going to be cut into strips eventually.

- Decorated wire, in valentine colors, 4 to 6 feet, total.

299

- String or ribbon, in valentine colors, a couple feet total.

- Ruler.

- Pencil.

- 6 paperclips

- Paper cutter or scissors.

- Stapler and staples.

Fold an eight and a half inch by 11-inch piece of cardstock in half lengthways. Measure and mark a one-inch strip from the fold out to the edge; cut it with a paper cutter or scissors. Repeat this for all of the paper.

The folded part of each strip will be the point of the heart; the loose ends will become the two humps. For each strip, measure a quarter inch from each end, marking a line across the strip. Punch two holes, a ways apart, along the lines you just drew on both ends. This will give you a total of four holes; two at each end.

Measure down two inches from the open end of each strip and mark across it again. Punch two more holes, through both layers of the strip.

Now you're ready to start making the heart humps. For each strip, separate the two ends and curve them inward and down toward the point. Carefully staple these open ends together, between the edge of the paper and the holes you just punched. Don't worry if your hearts look a little "fat"; we'll take care of that in a minute.

Lay your hearts out, side to side, on a flat surface, with the humps pointing toward you. Starting at one end, thread your wire through the top side hole of the first heart, through the stapled- together pieces, and out the other side. Repeat this process for each heart. Wrap the end of the wire around a paperclip so the hearts won't slip off the end. Flip the string of hearts over and repeat the process with another piece of wire, threading through the other hump-side holes.

When you're finished, bend the wire ends toward each other, making a loose circle with the heart points toward the center of the wreath. Tighten the wire until the hearts are snugly arranged in a circle, then twist the ends of the back wire together, followed by the ends of the front wire. Twist all four wires together to make a small hanging loop, and then cut off any excess.

Take two pieces of string or ribbon and cinch together the points of the hearts, threading through the holes, just like you did for the outer rim. Tie the ends of each string in a square knot when you're finished, and cut off any excess.

Patriotic Circle Fans

We have many patriotic holidays in the USA, such as the Fourth of July and Memorial Day. This craft allows you to create decoration you can use for Fourth of July and reuse for Memorial Day, Veterans Day, etc. You can hang them on the wall or on your front porch.

You will need:

- 8-1/2 by 11-inch decorative paper (scrapbook or origami paper) for small fans.

- 12-by-12-inch decorative paper for large fans.

- Stapler and staples.

- Ruler.

- Hot glue and gun.

- Scissors.

- Star cookie cutter.

- Cardstock.

- Pencil.

- String.

- Small dowel rod.

To make a small circle fan, take two sheets of paper and cut them in half, lengthwise. Fold the paper back and forth, making identical three quarter inch pleats.

To make the large circle fan take seven sheets of paper. Fold them in one-inch pleats.

Attach the small sheets together, end to end, using staples or glue. Close the circle by cinching in the middle to make a circular fan and glue or staple the edges together.

Trace the star cookie cutter with a pencil on your cardstock and cut out the star. Glue this to the center of the circular fan. Then, take a small piece of dowel rod and hot glue it to the back of the circular fan. I actually used two pieces glued in a cross shape and glued these to the center of the circular fan. Wrap string around the dowels once the glue dries and tie it in a loop to hang your fan.

Patriotic Jar Luminaries

The glow of luminaries creates a warm welcoming light along any walk or driveway. These are very easy to make and look great during patriotic summer evenings.

You will need:

- Glass jars – large pickle jars or canning jars work well. Remove any labels.

- Small American flags made of fabric (do not use plastic flags; they melt).

- Spray adhesive.

- Mod Podge and a brush.

- Sand.

- Votive candle.

Remove the stick from the flag and spread it face side down on a protected surface. Spray the back of the flag with spray adhesive and attach it to the outside of the jar, smoothing out any wrinkles and air bubbles. If your jar is bigger around than the flag is long, you may want to wrap a second flag around the rest of the jar. Cover the flag with a coat of Mod Podge, being careful not to get any on the jar outside of the flag area. Let it dry completely before proceeding.

Pour a generous inch of sand into the bottom of the jar and set a votive candle atop the sand. Light the candle and the flag will glow on the outside of the jar.

Peppermint Bowls

You make these cute little bowls out of the round, red and white peppermint hard candies that appear on shelves during Christmas. They can also be used on Valentine's Day, or any day you want to add a pop of color. You will need a heat-proof bowl for this project; I use a six-inch metal bowl.

You will need:

Cookie sheet covered with parchment paper.

Heat-proof bowl.

Vegetable oil.

18 peppermint candies, unwrapped.

Scissors.

Hotpads.

Line a cookie sheet with parchment paper and grease the outside of a bowl with vegetable oil. Preheat the oven to 275 degrees Fahrenheit. Set one candy in the center of the parchment paper on the cookie sheet and put it into the oven for two and a half minutes, or until it looks shiny.

Remove this from the oven and place six candies around the center one so that the sides are touching. Put the cookie sheet back in the oven for four to five minutes and remove when the candies start to soften, but do not melt. Place 11 more candies around the six, touching their neighbors, and return this to the oven for seven minutes. Remove from the oven and cool slightly.

Trim the parchment paper so it is close to the candies. Use a hot pad to flip the warm candies onto the greased bowl, centering it on base of bowl. Press the candies down until they take on the shape of the bowl. Let the candies rest and cool for at least five minutes.

Carefully remove the parchment paper from the candies and slide them off of the supporting bowl. Your peppermint bowl should retain its shape. Let it cool completely before moving it or touching it; you want to avoid making fingerprints on the bowl.

Ribbon Christmas Tree Ornament

These look nicely rustic; I prefer to use plaid or checked ribbon.

You will need:

- Twigs about the size of a pencil.

- Clippers.

- Ruler.

- Narrow green and red and ribbon.

- Button for the star at the top of the tree.

- Glue gun and glue.

- Twine.

- Scissors.

Cut six separate pieces of ribbon about four inches long. When you tie the ribbons to the twig, you will want equal amounts of ribbon on each side of the knot . Tie your first ribbon on the twig about one and a half to two inches above the bottom of the twig. Put hot glue under the knot to hold it in place.

Move up the twig, gluing in place five more pieces of ribbon, spacing them an equal distance apart, with the last one about an inch from the top of the twig. Once the glue is dry, cut diagonally down both sides to make the triangular shape of a tree, from the shortest ribbon at the top to the widest at the bottom. Cut five inches of twine and make an inch and a half loop at the top. Place the loop at the top of the twig and bring the tail down the length of the twig. Hot glue the loop to the back of the top of the twig then wind the twine around the trunk, avoiding the ribbons, and glue all the way down. Glue a button at the top in front of the loop to serve as a star.

Salt Clay Snowman Keepsake Ornament

This ornament is cute and will serve as a charming way to record your child's footprint at this age.

You will need:

- Salt clay.

- Rolling pin.

- Wax paper.

- Butter knife.

- Cookie sheet covered with parchment paper.

- Acrylic paint in white, black, red, and orange.

- Skewer.

- Ribbon or twine.

Roll out the salt clay on wax paper with a rolling pin until it is a half-inch thick. I always roll it out on the floor, because you will be taking a footprint. Press the foot into the clay, making a deep indentation. Cut around the foot, leaving a one-inch border, and set your footprint on a parchment-covered cookie sheet. Poke a hole in the very top (where the heel is located) with a bamboo skewer. Bake at 300 degrees Fahrenheit for 30 minutes, then let the footprint cool to room temperature.

The head and hat are where the heel is, so paint a round ball of white at the base of the of heel, then paint the rest of the indentation white all the way to the toes. This will be the body of your snowman. Let it dry thoroughly before proceeding.

Paint a black top hat above the head and then make black eyes and a black mouth. Use orange to paint a carrot nose. Paint a red scarf around the snowman's neck and run a few more black charcoal dots for buttons down the body.

Let the paint dry completely before you run a ribbon or piece of twine through the hole at the top and tie it in a loop for hanging.

Paint Chip Easter Egg Garland

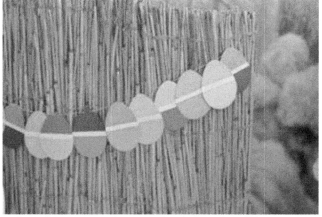

Use paint chips to make a string of spring-like Easter eggs.

Here is another craft that uses paint chips from the hardware store. The best to use is a four-colored paint chip.

You will need:

- Paint chips.

- Poster board, cut in an egg shape the desired length and width – this is a template.

- Pencil.

- Scissors.

- Hole punch.

- Waxed cotton string (use the waxed string because it resists movement of the eggs on the garland).

Cut out the egg template and place it on the back of the paint chip. Try to get all four colors in the egg. Cut out the egg. Punch two holes on each side of the egg a little higher than the middle, while holding with the small side on top. Repeat this process with as many eggs as you want to work with. String each egg onto the waxed cotton and move them so that the eggs are evenly spaced but touching. Hang on your mantle or over a door.

Unique Valentine In A Bottle

This is a unique way to tell your significant other you love him or her on Valentine's Day. You will roll up a message and stick it into a decorated bottle.

You will need:

- A glass or plastic bottle with a cap or cork.

- Scrapbook paper.

- Pen.

- Heart stickers.

- Heart confetti.

- Valentine-inspired ribbon.

- Thin ribbon.

- Scissors.

- Gift tag, pre-made or handmade.

Place heart stickers randomly on the outside of the bottle. Cut a square or rectangle of scrapbook paper that will fit in the bottle when rolled up. Write a Valentine's Day message on the white side of the paper and roll it up so the message is on the inside. Tie it with the thin ribbon to keep it rolled tightly. Drop the message into the bottle and pour in some heart-shaped confetti. Affix the cap or cork and tie several lengths of Valentine-inspired ribbon around the neck of the bottle. Write your valentine's name on the gift tag and affix it to the bottle.

Wine Glass Snow Globe Candleholder

I love these snow globe candleholders, made from long-stemmed wine glasses. Cheap wine glasses are easily located at thrift stores, yard sales, or a dollar store.

You will need:

- Long-stemmed wine glasses.

- A round piece of Styrofoam.

- Knife or craft knife.

- Glue suitable for Styrofoam.

- Holiday miniatures (snowmen, sleigh, reindeer, etc.).

- Cotton batting.

- Silk poinsettia pick with ribbon.

- Tray (optional).

- Votive candles or dripless pillar candles.

Cut the Styrofoam in a circle that's a little larger than the lip of the wine glass. Use Styrofoam-safe glue, as some glues will dissolve the Styrofoam. Glue your miniatures onto the Styrofoam and let the glue dry. Turn the glass upside down over the miniatures and center it over the Styrofoam, pressing the rim down firmly.

Cover the outside Styrofoam edge with a thin layer of cotton batting to make it look like snow. Tie a poinsettia pick around the stem of the wine glass just above the bowl of the glass. Cover the wire of the pick by wrapping a piece of ribbon in the same location and tying the ends into a bow. Set a candle atop the upturned base of the glass and you're ready to go. Your new holiday decoration looks great displayed on a mantle or on the dining room table.

Conclusion

I hope you had a lot of fun discovering fresh ways to unleash your creativity. By now you may be dreaming up ways to sell your crafts or use them to decorate your own home. Of course, you will have earmarked some to give as gifts to targeted friends, neighbors, and family members; everyone loves a homemade gift. You can make many of these crafts together as a family; the cooperation necessary in some of these projects can help your family communicate together and work more smoothly as a unit. You can use crafts to exercise your brain, teach your kids patience, and generally improve the mental health of all who participate.

The next step is to get crafting. Set up your own craft area and start gathering supplies. Set aside craft kits – preparing ahead of time everything you'll need in order to make a craft – for a rainy day with your kids. You can make up a quick craft kit for your next family gathering. Don't forget to set up what you need for your own crafting projects. After a difficult day, it can be therapeutic to have something you can work on with your own two hands. Choose your favorite craft from this book and start creating.

Thanks for reading.

If this book helped you or someone you know in any way then I invite you to leave a nice review right now. It would be greatly appreciated!

My Other Books

Be sure to check out my author page at:
https://www.amazon.com/author/susanhollister

UK: http://amzn.to/2qiEzA9

Or simply type my name into the search bar: Susan Hollister

Thank You

Made in the USA
Las Vegas, NV
10 February 2022

43673630R00171